The God Who Cares and Knows You

KAY ARTHUR
PETE DE LACY

HARVEST HOUSE PUBLISHERS
EUGENE, OREGON

Cover by Koechel Peterson & Associates, Inc., Minneapolis, Minnesota

THE GOD WHO CARES AND KNOWS YOU
Copyright © 2008 by Precept Ministries International
Published by Harvest House Publishers
Eugene, Oregon 97408
www.harvesthousepublishers.com

Library of Congress Cataloging-in-Publication Data

Arthur, Kay, 1933-
   The God who cares and knows you / Kay Arthur and Pete De Lacy.
      p. cm.—(The new inductive study series)
   ISBN 978-0-7369-2193-0 (pbk.)
   ISBN 978-0-7369-3588-3 (eBook)

   1. Bible. N.T. John—Textbooks. I. De Lacy, Pete. II. Title.
BS2616.A73 2008
226.50071—dc22

                                                                    2007019412

Printed in the United States of America

22 23 24 25 / BP-NI / 18 17 16 15 14

CONTENTS

∾∾∾∾

How to Get Started...

Reading directions is sometimes difficult and hardly ever enjoyable! Most often you just want to get started. Only if all else fails will you read the instructions. We understand, but please don't approach this study that way. These brief instructions are a vital part of getting started on the right foot! These few pages will help you immensely.

FIRST

As you study the Gospel of John, you will need four things in addition to this book:

1. A Bible that you are willing to mark in. The marking is essential. An ideal Bible for this purpose is *The New Inductive Study Bible (NISB)*. The *NISB* is in a single-column text format with large, easy-to-read type, which is ideal for marking. The margins of the text are wide and blank for note taking.

The *NISB* also has instructions for studying each book of the Bible, but it does not contain any commentary on the text, nor is it compiled from any theological stance. Its purpose is to teach you how to discern truth for yourself through the inductive method of study. (The various charts and maps that you will find in this study guide are taken from the *NISB*.)

Whichever Bible you use, just know you will need to mark in it, which brings us to the second item you will need...

2. A fine-point, four-color ballpoint pen or various colored fine-point pens that you can use to write in your Bible. Office supply stores should have those.

3. Colored pencils or an eight-color leaded Pentel pencil.

4. A composition book or a notebook for working on your assignments or recording your insights.

SECOND

1. As you study John, you will be given specific instructions for each day's study. These should take you between 20 and 30 minutes a day, but if you spend more time than this, you will increase your intimacy with the Word of God and the God of the Word.

If you are doing this study in a class and you find the lessons too heavy, simply do what you can. To do a little is better than to do nothing. Don't be an all-or-nothing person when it comes to Bible study.

Remember, anytime you get into the Word of God, you enter into more intensive warfare with the devil (our enemy). Why? Every piece of the Christian's armor is related to the Word of God. And our one and only offensive weapon is the sword of the Spirit, which is the Word of God. The enemy wants you to have a dull sword. Don't cooperate! You don't have to!

2. As you read each chapter, train yourself to ask the "5 W's and an H": who, what, when, where, why, and how. Asking questions like these helps you see exactly what the Word of God is saying. When you interrogate the text with the 5 W's and an H, you ask questions like these:

a. **What** is the chapter about?

b. **Who** are the main characters?

c. **When** does this event or teaching take place?

d. **Where** does this happen?

e. **Why** is this being done or said?

f. **How** did it happen?

3. Locations are important in a historical or biographical book of the Bible, so marking references to these in a distinguishable way will be helpful to you. I simply underline every reference to a location in green (grass and trees are green!) using my four-color ballpoint pen.

I also look up the locations on maps so I can put myself into context geographically. In the appendix of this book, you will find maps taken from the *NISB* that show you the geographical locations of Jesus' ministry. If you use these until you become familiar with these places, the Bible text will mean so much more to you.

4. You will be given certain key words to mark throughout this study. This is the purpose of the colored pencils and the colored pens. If you will develop the habit of marking your Bible in this way, you will find it will make a significant difference in the effectiveness of your study and in how much you remember.

A **key word** is an important word that the author uses repeatedly in order to convey his message to his readers. Certain key words will show up throughout the Gospel of John; others will be concentrated in specific chapters or segments of John. When you mark a key word, you should also mark its synonyms (words that mean the same thing in the context) and any pronouns *(he, his, she, her, it, we, they, us, our, you, their, them)* in the same way you have marked the key word. Also, mark each word the same way in all of its forms (such as *worship*, *worshippers*, and *worshipped*). We will give you suggestions for ways to mark key words in your daily assignments.

You can use colors or symbols or a combination of colors and symbols to mark words for easy identification. However, colors are easier to distinguish than symbols. When we use symbols, we keep them very simple. For example, you could draw a red heart around the word *love* and shade the inside of the heart like this: love .

When marking key words, mark them in a way that is easy for you to remember.

If you devise a color-coding system for marking key words throughout your Bible, then when you look at the pages of your Bible, you will see instantly where a key word is used.

You might want to make yourself a bookmark listing the words you want to mark along with their colors and/or symbols. We will mention some specific key words to watch for in each chapter of John, but you might consider watching out for these and marking them from the beginning:

Word, Jesus, Jesus Christ, Lamb of God, Son of God, Son of man

the Christ (Jesus is the Christ, but you'll see why we want you to mark this in a different way.)

Father

Spirit

life, live

sign

believe

born, born again

eternal life

love

true, truth

world

sin

5. A JOHN AT A GLANCE chart is included in the appendix. As you complete your study of each chapter, record the main theme of that chapter under the appropriate chapter number. The main theme of a chapter is what the chapter deals with the most. It may be a particular subject or teaching.

If you will fill out the JOHN AT A GLANCE chart as you progress through the study, you will have a complete synopsis of John when you are finished. If you have a *New Inductive Study Bible,* you will find the same chart in your Bible (page 1756). If you record your chapter themes there, you will have them for a ready reference.

6. Always begin your study with prayer. As you do your part to handle the Word of God accurately, you must remember that the Bible is a divinely inspired book. The words that you are reading are truth, given to you by God so you can know Him and His ways more intimately. These truths are divinely revealed.

> For to us God revealed them through the Spirit; for the Spirit searches all things, even the depths of God. For who among men knows

the thoughts of a man except the spirit of the man which is in him? Even so the thoughts of God no one knows except the Spirit of God (1 Corinthians 2:10-11).

Therefore ask God to reveal His truth to you as He leads and guides you into all truth. He will if you will ask.

7. Each day when you finish your lesson, meditate on what you saw. Ask your heavenly Father how you should live in light of the truths you have just studied. At times, depending on how God has spoken to you through His Word, you might even want to write LFL ("Lessons for Life") in the margin of your Bible and then, as briefly as possible, record the lesson for life that you want to remember.

THIRD

This study is set up so that you have an assignment for every day of the week—so that you are in the Word daily. If you work through your study in this way, you will find it more profitable than doing a week's study in one sitting. Pacing yourself this way allows time for thinking through what you learn on a daily basis!

The seventh day of each week differs from the other six days. The seventh day is designed to aid group discussion; however, it's also profitable if you are studying this book individually.

The "seventh" day is whatever day in the week you choose to finish your week's study. On this day, you will find a verse or two for you to memorize and STORE IN YOUR HEART. Then there is a passage to READ AND DISCUSS. This will help you focus on a major truth or major truths covered in your study that week.

To assist those using the material in a Sunday school class or a group Bible study, there are QUESTIONS FOR

Discussion or Individual Study. Even if you are not doing this study with anyone else, answering these questions would be good for you.

If you are in a group, be sure every member of the class, including the teacher, supports his or her answers and insights from the Bible text itself. Then you will be handling the Word of God accurately. As you learn to see what the text says and compare Scripture with Scripture, the Bible explains itself.

Always examine your insights by carefully observing the text to see what it *says*. Then, before you decide what the passage of Scripture *means,* make sure that you interpret it in the light of its context. Scripture will never contradict Scripture. If it ever seems to contradict the rest of the Word of God, you can be certain that something is being taken out of context. If you come to a passage that is difficult to understand, reserve your interpretations for a time when you can study the passage in greater depth.

The purpose of the Thought for the Week is to share with you what we consider to be an important element in your week of study. We have included it for your evaluation and, hopefully, for your edification. This section will help you see how to walk in light of what you learned.

Books in the New Inductive Study Series are survey courses. If you want to do a more in-depth study of a particular book of the Bible, we suggest you do a Precept Upon Precept Bible study course on that book. You may obtain more information on these courses by contacting Precept Ministries International at 800-763-8280, visiting our website at www.precept.org, or filling out and mailing the response card in the back of this book.

FINDING PURPOSE AND MEANING IN YOUR LIFE

Are you looking for purpose and meaning in your life? Is your life messed up? Are you trying to discover who you are and where you're going in life? These questions plague many people, so you're not alone if you're searching too. But where do you find answers? Is there a book of answers? An author who knows? Who? So many books by so many authors are available...how do you decide which one is right?

What if God can give you purpose and meaning even if you or someone else has messed up your life? What if He can show you how to live—regardless of your situation or circumstances? And what if He promised to love and care for you and give you the incomparable gift of eternal life so you can know for certain that the very moment you die, you will find yourself in His presence to live with Him forever as His dear child?

Surely you'd want to know this kind of God and find out how you can have a personal relationship with Him—a God who cares this much about you, whoever you are and wherever you've been—wouldn't you?

Well, my friend, that's what this book is all about. It's designed to help you know and understand the Bible so you can see for yourself what it says about God, what it says about you, and what it says about becoming a part of God's family.

Are you thirsty for meaning, my friend? Have you found anything that satisfies the deep emptiness and longing within? Has your religion satisfied you? Have you considered coming to Jesus—no matter what?

FROM DEATH TO LIFE

Do you ever feel dead? You know what I mean. You know you're physically alive, but on the inside you feel dead. You feel as if no life is there, and you wish there were. Perhaps you feel absolutely numb—nothing can make you happy, nothing gives you a high, nothing even gives you a low—as if you were in a state of anesthesia.

You can have hope, Beloved. A Light is shining that can lead you out of that deadness and into life.

DAY ONE

Some books of the Bible clearly state why they were written—this one, for example! So let's begin our study by reading John 20:30-31 and recording its purpose.

Now read John 1, noting the main characters. Which two are mentioned most?

You'll see the author emphasize subjects by repeating key words and phrases. You'll be marking many of these words and phrases throughout John, so a good technique is to record them and how you plan to mark them on a 3 x 5 card and use this as a bookmark. Doing this from lesson to lesson will help you mark consistently and save time.

Now read through John 1:1-18 again and mark *Word*. You may want to mark it yellow and add a purple underline and cross like this: **Word**.

DAY TWO

Now read John 1:1-18 again, marking pronouns referring to the Word the same way you marked *Word*. Read carefully to make sure the pronouns refer to the Word, not someone or something else! (Pronouns substitute for nouns—in this context you'll see words like *Him, His, He,* and in other places, *it.*)

Read John 1:1-18 again, this time marking synonyms for *Word*. (Synonyms are words that mean the same thing.)

DAY THREE

Today observe the verses in which you marked *Word* and its pronouns and synonyms in John 1:1-18. Make a list of what you learned from the text.

Now let's relate what we learned so far to John's purpose (20:30-31), which you read on day one. Has God given any signs to show that Jesus is the Son of God—that is to say, that Jesus is God? What does John 1:1-18 say about Jesus that you can relate to John 20:30-31?

DAY FOUR

Review day one. Who's the other main character of John 1? Read through John 1:1-18 again, marking this person, if you want, with a squiggly underline like this: **John**.

Now list everything that you learned about him.

DAY FIVE

Read John 1:19-51 and mark every reference to *Jesus Christ* the same way you marked *Word*. Don't miss pronouns and synonyms like *Lamb of God* and *man*.

Now read John 1:19-51 again and mark every reference to *John*.

DAY SIX

Today, add all you learned in 1:19-51 about Jesus and John to the lists you made from verses 1-18.

Finally, think about all you have seen this week and determine the main subject of this chapter. Write this out as a theme for John 1 and record it on JOHN AT A GLANCE in the appendix.

DAY SEVEN

 Store in your heart: John 1:1,14

Read and discuss: John 1:1-27; 20:30-31

QUESTIONS FOR DISCUSSION OR INDIVIDUAL STUDY

- What is the purpose of the Gospel of John?

- What evidence do you see in John 1:1-18 that Jesus is the Son of God?

∾ Discuss how to become a child of God. What is the result of believing?

∾ Who is the witness in John 1:1-27? What function does witnessing involve?

∾ What's the significance of signs being done in the presence of the disciples (20:30)?

∾ What application can you make to your own life? Are you a child of God? How do you know?

∾ How does this week's study motivate you to share what you learned with others?

THOUGHT FOR THE WEEK

Perhaps you're unhappy and feel trapped by circumstances in your life. Nothing in life excites you. You just feel dead. And the thing is, you may actually *be* spiritually dead. You need to know that being spiritually dead in this life is like hell because you keep looking for something that's going to make you happy, something that's going to touch you, something that's going to make you come alive. But you don't realize that it's some One.

Maybe you've gone to psychologists or even psychiatrists seeking answers but haven't found them. Maybe you've tried killing the numbness with pills, alcohol, or drugs. But even these don't take away the deadness, the feeling of no answers, no hope.

John says he wrote his Gospel so that we might believe that Jesus is the Christ, the Son of the living God, and that believing we might have life in His name. That life is the only life with true hope. When you and I believe that Jesus is the Christ, the Son of God, we get life. Before this, if we feel dead, it's because we are. We were all spiritually still-born because of trespasses and sins (Ephesians 2:1). So if you haven't been made alive in Christ, feeling dead is legitimate. And if you have been made alive but still feel dead, Jesus says there's more to the life you have; there's abundant life (John 10:10). Whatever's missing, leaving us feeling dead, He supplies.

To achieve his purpose, John is going to show us signs that Jesus performed in the presence of His disciples. Not every sign, but the signs that the world needs to see in order to know that Jesus is the Christ.

John 1:1 tells us that the Word has always been—He was in the beginning. We also learn that He was with God—so we know He's distinct in some way from God. And what else is He? The Lamb of God, according to verse 29. And there we learn His name—Jesus.

And He is life. So if you feel dead, where do you find life? In Jesus Christ. And what is that life? It's the Light that enlightens every man. In other words, everyone is born with some sort of a hope for eternal life. People know somebody is "out there" apart from them—some source of light and life. They know they need to bow to someone. You say, "Not me! I don't believe in a God. I believe *I'm* god!" Then you do believe there's a god, and that god is you—and that will cause trouble.

So to review, we see that Jesus is the Light. We see that He's life. We see that He had a witness named John the Baptist. Jesus was born a Jew and came to Jews who did not receive Him, who did not believe. But is that the end of the story?

No! He gives the right to become children of God to those who believe in His name—anyone who believes, including you and me.

John's purpose is to declare that if we believe in His name, we are going to have life. If we believe that Jesus is the

Christ, if we believe that He's the Son of God, we're going to have life in His name. Some people ask, if Jesus is God, why doesn't everybody believe in Him? If Jesus is the Savior of the world, why doesn't everybody receive Him? The reason is that even though the Light shines in the darkness, the darkness does not comprehend it.

How does John describe the ones who receive the true Light? We read that they are born not of blood, not of will of the flesh, nor of the will of man, but of God. But what does this mean? It means you aren't naturally born a Christian. You become one when you're born *again*. When you're born the first time, you're physically alive but spiritually dead. But you come alive spiritually in Jesus when you receive Him. You receive eternal life, and He gives you truth, which sets you free. Truth gives you life because Jesus is the way, the truth, and the life.

Jesus once turned around and asked His disciples, "Who do you say that I am?" People had diverse opinions about Him then as they do today, but Jesus always asks, "Who do *you* say that I am?" Other people's opinions about Jesus Christ really don't matter; what God says is what counts. Some say He's a great teacher, "the man upstairs," a great philosopher, or a good man, but they don't believe He is God. But if He is just a man and teaches that He's God, then He's a bad teacher. But the Bible teaches that He is the Son of God in a way that no one else is or ever could be.

If you have Christ, you have everything you'll ever need. Why? Because Jesus is in you, and He is the Light, He is life, He is God, and He is the Lamb of God who takes away the sins of the world.

The key is that the Word of God became flesh and dwelt among us—He was given to us and sacrificed for us so that we might live. So here is the Word of God. Here is the One that has life. John introduces this Jesus in his first chapter. No mention of signs yet—he simply lays down that this is Jesus, the Son of God. He is the One on whom angels of God descend (verse 51) because He is also the Son of Man. And you can thank Him for becoming flesh because He did so to take away the sins of the world.

Are you loaded with guilt? Do you feel dead on the inside, my friend? Oh, listen very, very carefully. Help and hope are available for you.

BORN AGAIN OR RELIGIOUS?

If someone believes that Jesus is the Christ, the Son of God, is he religious, or is he born again? What's the difference? Does it matter? What does the Word of God say?

DAY ONE

Read through John 2 today. As you read, mark references to time. When the Word of God gives us time indicators, we need to pay attention. We don't often find specific hours, days, or years, but we do see sequences of events. In John, for example, marking references to the feasts of Israel will help you see the passage of time and sequence of events in Jesus' ministry. Mark these with a clock, like this:.

Marking locations is also helpful. Here in John, locations help us understand the sequence of events in Jesus' ministry. Double underline these in green.

When you finish marking references to time and locations in John 2, go back and mark the same things in John 1. Refer to the map in the appendix to identify these locations. Throughout this study, you might note time sequences on this map by sequentially numbering the places as they appear from chapter to chapter.

DAY TWO

Read through John 2 again today, marking the word *sign*[1] like this: **sign** . (Don't forget to mark *signs* the same way.) Also mark *believed*. John's use of *sign* and *believed* both support John's purpose expressed in 20:30-31.

Read John 20:30-31 and mark these key words. Don't miss the pronoun referring to *signs*.

DAY THREE

Read John 2 once more today, and we'll finish our study of this chapter. As you read, look for main events. In the margin of your Bible, note each one. For example, at John 2:1 you could write, "Wedding at Cana."

Now, let's look at the first sign Jesus performed. What was it? Where did He do it? Who saw it? What was the result?

In the margin of your Bible, note the first sign. You could simply write, "Jesus' first sign." Now look for other signs mentioned in John 2 and ask the 5 W's and H about them just as we did for the first sign.

Make a list of what you learned about the signs.

Finally, determine the theme of John 2 and record it on JOHN AT A GLANCE in the appendix.

DAY FOUR

Read John 3 today to get the flow of the chapter and the events in it. As you did for John 2, mark references to time and location and note in the margin of your Bible the events of this chapter.

Now read John 3:1-21 again, marking the same key words that you marked in John 2. Did you see any other key (repeated) words in this passage? List them.

Where was Jesus when this confrontation occurred? If you're not sure, read John 2:23.

DAY FIVE

We're going to focus on John 3:1-21 again today, marking the key words *born,*[2] *born again,* and *eternal life.*[3] If these are among the words you listed yesterday, you're already learning how to spot key words!

Now let's examine what we've learned. What is John 3:1-21 about? Who is Nicodemus? Why did he come to Jesus? What did Jesus tell Nicodemus he had to do in order to see the kingdom of God? Write your answers in your notebook.

Now list in your notebook all you learned about *believe* (and, of course, *believed* and *believes*), *born, born again,* and *eternal life.*

As your last assignment, mark references to *God* in John 3:1-21 with a triangle. Then list what you learn about Him. Remember to ask the 5 W's and H as you make your list.

DAY SIX

For our last day of study this week, read John 3:22-36. Mark the key words on your bookmark, and mark references to time and locations.

Who are the key characters in this passage? Did you see any other words that are key to understanding this passage? Choose a way to mark them too.

Now list what you learned from marking them.

How does this passage relate to John 1?

Don't forget to determine a theme for John 3 and record it on JOHN AT A GLANCE in the appendix.

DAY SEVEN

 Store in your heart: John 3:3,16

Read and discuss: John 2:1-11; 3:1-21

QUESTIONS FOR DISCUSSION OR INDIVIDUAL STUDY

∾ Whom or what do you worship?

∾ Are you a Christian? Do you have religion without a personal, intimate relationship with God the Father? Deep in your heart, do you know you can call Him "Father" because you're His child, born of the Spirit?

∾ If you're not a Christian, how does your god compare to the One you've seen so far in your study of John?

∾ What did you learn about being born again and about eternal life?

∾ Discuss the first sign Jesus performed. What does it show you about Him?

∾ Review John's purpose and how it relates to signs, belief, and eternal life.

ᖆ Summarize the main events of these two chapters and what they teach you about salvation.

ᖆ Discuss how you can remember the chapter themes you listed on JOHN AT A GLANCE.

THOUGHT FOR THE WEEK

When my life was a total mess and I knew that I couldn't do anything about it, that I couldn't change myself regardless of how hard I tried, I cried out to God in ignorance, *If I could just start life over…if I could just be born again…* That's when it all began to happen, and I was born again—I was absolutely transformed.

Unless one is born again, he cannot enter the kingdom of heaven. Nicodemus, a ruler of the Jews, was a religious man. Yet he came to Jesus Christ because of signs he saw, and he said to Him, "No one can do these signs that You do unless God is with him." Jesus cuts right through all of his religiosity, right through to the heart of Nicodemus' concern, and this is what He says: "Truly, truly I say unto you, unless one is born again he cannot see the kingdom of God."

Nicodemus asks the question anyone would ask: "How can a man be born when he is old? He cannot enter a second time into his mother's womb and be born, can he?" And he's thinking, *Okay, I have to be born again. I was born from my mother's womb. I can't get in there again and be born because I'm a man now, so how can this be?* Jesus answers that men must be born of water *and* of the Spirit to enter the kingdom of God. So for us to enter the kingdom of God, for us to become new creatures in Christ Jesus, for us to become children of God, we have to be born again.

What does Jesus mean when He says, "That which is born of the flesh is flesh"? He means that human beings have babies! What does "that which is born of the Spirit is spirit" mean? This is the born *again* part. John compares spirit to wind: "The wind blows where it wishes and you hear the sound of it, but do not know where it comes from and where it is going; so is everyone who is born of the Spirit." The Spirit is like the wind. You don't know where it's coming from, and you don't know where it's going; you simply see and hear its effects in trees, on flags, and in your hair.

How does this rebirth happen? From this point on, John's Gospel explains how to be born of the Spirit. We're born of the Spirit by believing in the Lord Jesus Christ.

Now let's look at the role the Holy Spirit plays in our salvation. Ephesians 1:13 says, "In Him [Christ], you also, after listening to the message of the truth, the gospel of your salvation—having also believed, you were sealed in Him with the Holy Spirit of promise." When we are born again, God seals us in Jesus by putting the Holy Spirit in us. The Holy Spirit is the seal, the guarantee of the redemption of this purchased possession. The Holy Spirit "is given as a pledge of our inheritance, with a view to the redemption of God's own possession, to the praise of His glory" (Ephesians 1:14). So what do you do? You hear the message of salvation, and after you believe, you receive the Holy Spirit.

Paul calls Him "the Holy Spirit of promise" (Ephesians 1:13). God's promise to the nation of Israel becomes ours when we believe: "Moreover, I will give you a new heart and put a new spirit within you; and I will remove the heart of stone from your flesh and give you a heart of flesh. I will put My Spirit within you and cause you to walk in My statutes, and you will be careful to observe My ordinances" (Ezekiel 36:26-27).

When you believe, God puts His Spirit in you, sealing you in Him, and that guarantees you are a child of God. So you can know this, precious one: If you've been born again, God wanted that to happen. You're not born again because you were born a Christian. You're not born again because of your bloodline. You go to heaven because God decided to give you a new birth. The Spirit of God brings you to God. He causes us "to be born again to a living hope through the resurrection of Jesus Christ from the dead" (1 Peter 1:3).

Paul distinguishes between flesh and spirit in 1 Corinthians 15:45-49:

> It is written, "The first man, Adam, became a living soul." The last Adam became a life-giving spirit. However, the spiritual is not first, but the natural; then the spiritual. The first man is from the earth, earthy; the second man is from heaven. As is the earthy, so also are those who are earthy; and as is the heavenly, so also are those who are heavenly. Just as we have borne the image of the earthy, we will also bear the image of the heavenly.

So because of our physical birth, we bear the image of the fleshly and earthly, but these images are never going to get us to heaven. We have to bear the image of the heavenly. We bear the image of the heavenly by the indwelling Holy Spirit, who comes when we believe in the Lord Jesus Christ.

This is what Jesus is referring to when He talks about being born again. Just being religious isn't going to do it; good intentions to please God are not enough. You have to be born of the Spirit because "if anyone does not have the Spirit of Christ, he does not belong to Him" (Romans 8:9).

The question, my friend, is this: Have you been born again?

YOUR PURPOSE IN LIFE

What's your goal—your driving passion? Is it satisfying? If you were about to die, would you know you had finished your spiritual course successfully? If not, we need to talk.

DAY ONE

Read John 4:1-42 today, noting where Jesus goes. Watch for time phrases. Also mark geographical locations as you have in previous chapters and find them on the map in the appendix.

In the margin, write the name of the city where the events of John 4:1-42 happen.

Mark in a distinctive way or color the key words *woman, worship, eternal life,*[4] and *believe.* Don't forget to include any pronouns, synonyms, or different forms of the key words. There's no need to add *woman* or *worship* to your bookmark, as these are key words only in chapter 4.

DAY TWO

Find Samaria on the map in the appendix. Also note where Jesus was coming from and where He was going.

31

Read John 4:9 and record what you learn about the Jews' relationship to the Samaritans.

The Samaritans were most likely racially mixed. After Assyria took the northern kingdom of Israel captive, they left some of the poorest Jews (from ten of Israel's twelve tribes) in the land and sent people from other lands to live there too. Some of these intermarried, and their religious beliefs blended Jewish and pagan thought. Living in a region called Samaria, they were known as Samaritans. Because their religion mixed pagan elements with Judaism, the purebred Jews didn't like them.

Yesterday you marked *worship*. List in your notebook in two columns what you learned about Samaritan and Jewish worship.

In John 4, who compares Samaritan worship to Jewish worship and then explains *true* worship? Can His word be trusted? (Read John 14:6 if you have any doubt.)

According to verse 22, where does salvation come from?

We saw in John 1:1-2 that the Word was God and was with God in the beginning. But we saw too that He was made flesh and became man (1:14). What was Jesus' nationality?

He was born a Jew. The Jews, His own people, for the most part did not receive Him (John 1:11). Maybe, my friend, you can relate to Jesus. If so, you know He understands what you are going through.

Read John 4:25-29. Who were the Samaritans looking for? How did Jesus respond? How did the woman respond to what Jesus said?

List in your notebook what you learned from marking *believe*. Note who believes, what they believe, and why.

DAY THREE

Read John 4:1-42 again. Be sure you've marked every reference to *woman*, including pronouns.

Make a list of everything you learned about this woman.

What do you learn about Jesus' attitude toward women from this passage?

Was this immoral Samaritan woman important to Jesus? How do you know? How did He treat her? What did He want for her?

Were Jesus' disciples surprised that He talked with this woman? What does this tell you about how women were treated at the time?

Was it God's will for Jesus to treat the Samaritan woman the way He did? How do you know?

DAY FOUR

Today read John 4:43-54. Note where Jesus goes next and mark it the same way you've marked locations before. Mark the words *sign*[5] and *believe*.

Record your theme for John 4 on JOHN AT A GLANCE in the appendix.

DAY FIVE

Read John 5 and mark the following key words: *Father, live (life)*,[6] *testimony*,[7] and *believe*.

Mark *God* and *Father* with a triangle and color it yellow. (Be careful when you mark pronouns that refer to the Father—it's easy to get confused and mark ones that refer to the Son.)

Look back through chapter 5 and see if you need to mark time phrases or geographical locations. Check the map in the appendix.

DAY SIX

Read John 5:15-47 and mark every reference to *Jesus,* including pronouns and synonyms, such as *Son.*

Now list what you learn about God the Father and God the Son.

Now, Beloved, take a few moments to think about the relationship between the Father and the Son. Remember that John 1:18 told us that Jesus came to explain the Father. How did Jesus explain the Father in John 5?

How should we live if we want to explain God the Father and God the Son to people?

Make a list of what you learn about *life* in John 5.

Determine a theme for John 5 and record it on JOHN AT A GLANCE.

DAY SEVEN

 Store in your heart: John 4:35

Read and discuss: John 4:1-42; 5

QUESTIONS FOR DISCUSSION OR INDIVIDUAL STUDY

- ∾ Discuss Samaritan worship. How did it differ from Jewish worship?

- ∾ What is *true* worship?

- ∾ How did Jesus deal with the woman?

- ∾ Compare Jesus' attitude toward the Samaritan woman with His disciples' attitude.

- ∾ Why did Jesus go through Samaria? Was it the only way to go from Jerusalem to Galilee, or was Jesus there for another reason?

- ∾ What did you learn from marking *believe*?

- ∾ What did you learn in chapter 5 about God the Father and God the Son?

THOUGHT FOR THE WEEK

What is your goal in life? What is your driving passion? If your life were ending, would you look back and say, "It's okay; I did what I was supposed to do!" So many people are driving, pushing, and straining to do more, but they get to the end dissatisfied.

This doesn't mean God wants to move you out of your occupation or position when He saves you. Rather, he wants you to know that wherever you are (even in your own "Samaria"), you have a new purpose: to do His will. John 4 and 5 take place at two different times, and John uses both of them to show the relationship Jesus Christ had with His Father. As you look at that relationship, you're going to learn about your own walk with the Father. If you walk this way with Him, you won't feel incomplete at the end of your life.

John 4 records Jesus going to Samaria. The woman He meets comes to know Him and leaves her water pot. She runs into the city and tells some men, "Come, see a man who told me all the things that I have done." Meanwhile… The disciples were urging Him, saying, "Rabbi, eat."

> But He said to them, "I have food to eat that you do not know about."
>
> So the disciples were saying to one another, "No one brought Him anything to eat, did he?"
>
> Jesus said to them, "My food is to do the will of Him who sent Me and to accomplish His work. Do you not say, 'There are yet four months, and then comes the harvest'? Behold, I say to you, lift up your eyes and look on the fields, that they are white for harvest."

God wants you and me to lift up our eyes and look at the harvest. Why? Because He's got a harvesting job for us in fields that are white (ready), and if we don't do it, we're going to be sorry when we see Him face-to-face. Jesus told His disciples that His food (meat) was to do the will of God, and we should stop and think about the context in which He said this.

Where's the Samaritan woman? Remember, she went into a city to tell people to come meet the man who told her all the things she had done. So she's gone, and His disciples are there. Their focus is on food, and they think, *Surely Jesus has to be hungry.* Jesus says, "Lift up your eyes and look on the fields that they are white for harvest." Now, when fields were white for harvest, they were overripe—in other words, they should have been harvested a long time ago. This is an important analogy. What are we here for? Why have we come to know the Lord Jesus Christ? What happened that is so valuable? Do we have something to tell people?

Let's look at what's happening in the Gospel of John. God is showing us a pattern. Remember, John was written so unbelievers would come to faith in Jesus the Messiah (Christ), the Son of God, and have life in His name. And what does Jesus do to convince men to believe? He does miracles—signs. In chapter 3, what brought Nicodemus to Jesus Christ? A sign! Here in chapter 4, we see Jesus doing miraculous signs again.

After His encounter with the Samaritan woman, Jesus stays in Samaria for two days. Why? John 4:39 says, "From that city many of the Samaritans believed in Him because of the word of the woman who testified, 'He told me all things that I have done.'" When this woman believed, she didn't think, *I'm going to keep this to myself!* Instead, she took the good news, ran into the city, and shared it with many people. Jesus' knowledge of her secret life identified Him as the Christ, the Anointed One of God. Accordingly, she told these people the Messiah had come. They came out to hear Jesus because they believed her word.

And this was just the beginning. Verse 40 says, "So when the Samaritans came to Jesus, they were asking Him to stay with them; and He stayed there two days." He didn't just walk through; He stayed with people the Jews considered enemies. And according to verse 41, "Many more believed because of His word." That's really the way it ought to be. We share the Word of God. We share our testimony, but then we lead people out of their cities to meet Christ themselves by getting them into His Word. That's what this Bible study is all about. "And they were saying to the woman, 'It is no longer because of what you said that we believe, for we have heard for ourselves and know that this One is indeed the Savior of the world'" (verse 42).

From there Jesus went to Galilee, and the Galileans received Him. One of the towns He visited was Cana.

In Capernaum, a royal official who knew about Jesus and heard that He was in the area went to ask Him to heal his dying son.

> Jesus said to him, "Go; your son lives." The man believed the word that Jesus spoke to him and started off. As he was now going down, his slaves met him, saying that his son was living. So he inquired of them the hour when he began to get better. Then they said to him, "Yesterday at the seventh hour the fever left him." So the father knew that it was at that hour in which Jesus said to him, "Your son lives"; and he himself believed and his whole household.

These events show us something crucially important. If you want a complete life, one you won't be ashamed of when you see Jesus, your food has to be to do His will now. When Jesus knew the time of His death had come and He was approaching the Garden of Gethsemane, where He would be arrested, He stopped and prayed to the Father, saying, "I have finished the work which thou gavest me to do" (John 17:4 KJV). All His life He had to be about His Father's business.

From the time you get new life from Jesus, you too have one goal, my friend—to be about the Father's business, to do His will. The Father works, the Son worked, and you and I are to be at work. We need to be about our Father's business of harvesting fields white for harvest.

How did Jesus deal with Nicodemus in chapter 3? The first thing He said to that religious leader is this: "Unless one is born again he cannot see the kingdom of God." And so right away He addresses the point of interest, the point of need, the focal point of Nicodemus' life. Nicodemus is a ruler of the Jews, a teacher, a prominent Pharisee, so this is his interest. His profession is the kingdom of God.

When Jesus goes to Samaria and a woman approaches Him, she's coming to get water. So what does He say to the woman? He asks her for a drink, and then He says to her, "If you knew…who it is who says to you, 'Give me a drink,' you would have asked Him, and He would have given you living water." He deals entirely differently with the woman, but He still addresses her point of interest, her point of need.

The official from Capernaum comes to Him because his son is sick. In fact, the son is dying, so the official is focused on one thing, and that is his son. Jesus does not give him a long theological dissertation. He doesn't talk to him about living water or about entering the kingdom of heaven. Jesus meets him where he is, and He heals his son.

If you encounter someone who is sick, before you start doling out the gospel, you can simply say, "I'd love to pray for your child," or "I'd love to pray for you," or "I want you to know I'll be praying for you. I can't heal, but Jehovah Rapha (the healer) can. I know you're scared, and I know this is hard, but would you mind if I prayed with you right now?" Nine times out of ten, that person will respond, "I wouldn't mind at all. Thank you." So you come alongside and befriend that person, and then that person is listening and is ready to receive the gospel.

So we see three different people in three different circumstances, and Jesus, instead of going through a dissertation on the gospel, meets them where they are. What applies to bodies falling apart applies to marriages falling apart. Show people compassion first and then offer them answers—introducing them eventually to the One who has the answers and to a new life they can live. When you do this, precious one, you've got an open door for the gospel. Jesus always and only did those things that pleased His Father. The Son of God left us a pattern to follow.

And you and I become children of God when we believe on His name. So the Son of God models for the children of God how they are to live in relationship to the Father. Know this, my precious friend: He has many witnesses who testify that He is the Son of God, and you need to remember that someday you're going to stand before Him. What will it be like? Remember, my friend, that you will give an account. This is sure—there are enough witnesses to prove it. The rest of John 5 tells us that Jesus' works bore witness, John the Baptist bore witness, the Father bore witness, and the Word continues to bear witness that all of this is true. Who are you going to believe now?

WHERE WILL YOU GO?

My friend, do you ever feel like walking away from God? Do you ever feel as if the things God wants, the things He expects, and the things He commands are just too hard? *I think I'll walk away!* Oh my friend, don't! Where would you go?

DAY ONE

Read John 6 and mark every reference to *bread,* including synonyms and pronouns. Don't add it to your bookmark because this is a key term in this chapter only.

Also mark geographical locations and locate them on the map in the appendix you've done before. Remember to mark time references too. You've been marking *Passover,* but it's helpful to mark the feasts in special ways, perhaps writing their names in the margins of your Bible. For a better understanding of the feasts, look in the appendix at the chart called THE FEASTS OF ISRAEL.

DAY TWO

Read John 6 again today, marking these words: *life, eternal life,*[8] and *live* (if it refers to eternal life), *believe, flesh* (mark this the same way you marked *bread* yesterday), and *sign.*[9]

This will take some time because John 6 has 71 verses, so we'll call it a day. It's good to pore over the text again, letting these words of life soak deeply into your soul. Take your time and enjoy the journey.

DAY THREE

Today, make a list of what you learned from marking *sign* and *believe*.

DAY FOUR

Read through John 6:1-40 again. This time, watch how Jesus uses the signs of the fish and the loaves to teach the multitudes. What does He want them to see?

List everything you learn about the true *bread*, which comes down from heaven.

List everything you learn from marking *life* and its synonyms.

DAY FIVE

Read John 6:41-59 and mark *raise*. Then list what you learn about who is going to be raised on the last day.

When Jesus talks about eating His flesh and drinking His blood in John 6:51-58, do you think He's speaking figuratively? Why? What do you think He means? What point is He making? Think about the context of this chapter.

When Jesus talks about being raised up on the last day, is He implying one of a string of reincarnations in temporary forms (such as animals) or being brought back at a different level of attainment as some religions teach? To answer these questions, think about what you listed about who's going to be raised up on the last day, and then read John 5:24-29. Now write out your answer according to all you have seen in John. (By the time you get to the end of your study of the Gospel of John, you will have even greater insights into what happens to a born-again Christian when he or she dies.)

DAY SIX

Read John 6:60-71 and mark *Spirit*. According to this chapter, how did the crowd of followers respond to what Jesus said? How did the twelve respond?

What does Jesus say in this chapter about eternal life? What does this say about your future?

Read John 6:64-71 and mark every reference to *Judas*. Jesus chose Judas to be one of the twelve disciples. List your insights about him.

From a human perspective, if Judas could betray Jesus, could others who professed to be His disciples do the same? To put it another way, are all who say they're Christians true Christians? How do we know?

Beloved, from all you've seen, is it possible to have eternal life apart from Christ?

Don't forget to record a theme for John 6 on JOHN AT A GLANCE.

DAY SEVEN

Store in your heart: John 6:35

Read and discuss: John 6:26-69

QUESTIONS FOR DISCUSSION OR INDIVIDUAL STUDY

- ∞ What did you learn about the bread of life?

- ∞ Contrast the bread from heaven with earthly bread, such as the bread that fed the 5000 and the manna that fed the Jews in the wilderness.

- ∞ How is the bread of life related to eternal life?

- ∞ What did Jesus mean by eating His flesh and drinking His blood?

- ∞ Discuss what you learned about being raised up on the last day.

- ∞ How does someone come to the Son?

- ∞ Discuss how you can apply what you learned in John 6 to your life today.

THOUGHT FOR THE WEEK

Have you ever had a hard time believing God, a time when your plans were disrupted by circumstances and you saw no hope for their coming about? Did you doubt, thinking, *I can't do this. Can I run away?* If you had walked away, would you have been disobedient to God? Oh, definitely! And where would you have gone?

Jesus' disciples faced the same dilemma. So He asked, "Are you going to walk away too?" And they said, "Lord, to whom shall we go? You have the words of eternal life." You know that God said man doesn't live by bread alone but by every word that proceeds out of the mouth of God. I want you to know the words of God so that when you're tempted to walk away, you can say to yourself, *Where would I go? Jesus alone has the words of life.*

Sometimes Jesus' sayings are hard. Our circumstances can be hard too, but regardless of how much we want to quit...where else can we go? Jesus alone gives eternal life!

I want you to remember this. God's Word and His ways are not always easy to understand and accept. But our understanding is limited, so before the hard times come, we need to decide that we will see and do the work of God.

Now, what is the work of God?

According to John 6, 5000 hungry men (not counting women and children) gathered around Jesus. Jesus multiplied two fish and five loaves that a boy had for his lunch, and the whole multitude was fed—with 12 baskets of food left over. He was showing them that He was the God of exceeding abundance, who is able to do far more than we can ask or think.

What was the result of this sign? The people knew from Moses' prophecy that a Prophet was coming: "The LORD your God will raise up for you a prophet like me from among you, from your countrymen, you shall listen to him" (Deuteronomy 18:15).

After Jesus walked on the Sea of Galilee and crossed over to the other side the next day, the crowd found Him and asked Him how He got there. Jesus said, "Truly, truly, I say to you, you seek Me, not because you saw signs, but because you ate of the loaves and were filled." Then He said,

"Do not work for the food which perishes, but for the food which endures to eternal life, which the Son of Man will give to you, for on Him the Father, God, has set His seal."

Then the people asked, "What shall we do, so that we may work the works of God?" Jesus answered, "This is the work of God, that you believe in Him whom He has sent" (John 6:26-29). Sometimes believing in Him really is hard work because everything in your being is crying out to run away. You think, *I don't need this! I'm not going to stay; this is too much to ask.* It's hard work to hang on and say, *God, I'm going to believe You no matter what. Where would I go if I walked away?* But that's an important question for us to consider.

The people continue, "What then do You do for a sign, so that we may see, and believe You? What work do You perform? Our fathers ate manna in the wilderness; as it is written, 'He gave them bread out of heaven to eat.'" And Jesus said to them, "It is not Moses who has given you the bread out of heaven, but it is My Father who gives you the true bread out of heaven." He tells them He's the true bread: "The bread of God is that which comes down out of heaven, and gives life to the world."

The bread they ate satisfied them only for a day, but when you eat the flesh of the Son of man, when you make Christ an integral part of your life, when you acknowledge who He is, then you receive the Prophet, the Christ, the Promised One, the Son of God. He is one with the Father. He is life, and His life is the light of men. When you receive Him, you receive life, eternal life.

The people thought He was speaking of a physical kind of bread that would permanently satisfy hunger when they said, "Lord, always give us this bread." But Jesus quickly dispelled that thinking when He said, "I am the bread of life;

he who comes to Me will not hunger, and he who believes in Me will never thirst."

Jesus' claim to be the bread that came down out of heaven made the Jews grumble. They asked, "Is this not Jesus, the son of Joseph, whose father and mother we know? How does He now say, 'I have come down out of heaven'?" Then Jesus said, "Do not grumble among yourselves. No one can come to Me unless the Father who sent Me draws him; and I will raise him up in the last day" (verses 42-44).

Why is Jesus' statement so difficult for us to accept? The answer is that it shows us that we do not initiate our salvation. We're not the ones who decide! We discover that we come to Him because of His mercy, His grace, His drawing us to Himself. You may ask, "What if I want to come to Him and He won't take me?" Know this—you won't want this unless He changes your heart.

Jesus now continues explaining what He means when He says He's the bread of life: "I am the living bread that came down out of heaven; if anyone eats of this bread, he will live forever; and the bread also which I will give for the life of the world is My flesh" (verse 51). So what is He saying? We might paraphrase His words this way: "The bread that I'm going to give for the life of the world is this earthly body that I'm in—I'm going to offer it to God on the cross. No one will take it from Me; I'll lay it down to give My flesh for the life of the world."

Giving His flesh for the life of the world is connected with His death. Accordingly, it doesn't mean that eating His flesh and drinking His blood are physical actions. These were forbidden to the Jews, and Jesus would not break the Mosaic Law. Initially, though, this is confusing to them: "Then the Jews began to argue with one another, saying, 'How can this man give us His flesh to eat?'" (verse 52).

Where are they again? Down here on the physical level. Nicodemus asked, "How can I be born again? Crawl back into my mother's womb?" The woman at the well requested, "Give me this water so I'll never thirst." Jesus had replied that He is the water. Now He's saying His flesh is the bread, and the crowd is asking, "How can He give us His flesh to eat?"

He explains, "Truly, truly, I say to you, unless you eat the flesh of the Son of Man and drink His blood, you have no life in yourselves" (verse 53). Now where is life? In Christ alone. Life is not in another person who is dying. There's only One who *is* life, and that's Jesus.

Be sure to remember the context of this. Passover was near—when lambs were killed and eaten to commemorate how the blood of a slain lamb put on doorposts saved Israel's firstborn from death when they were in Egypt.

According to Matthew, Jesus said the cup and bread at the Passover meal are His body and blood to be shed for many, establishing the New Covenant (Matthew 26:26-28). In 1 Corinthians 11:25-26, Paul says with reference to taking communion, "In the same way He took the cup also after supper, saying, 'This cup is the new covenant in My blood; do this, as often as you drink it, in remembrance of Me.'" We don't *receive* Him in communion; we *remember* Him—specifically, what He did for us. "For as often as you eat this bread and drink the cup, you proclaim the Lord's death until He comes." The Lord's death for your sins, that is.

The Jews realized that Jesus' words were difficult to believe because they understood the concept of covenant. Some probably said, "Okay, we'll walk in covenant with You and share things with You. We'll believe You; we'll receive Your teachings." This was quite a commitment, but they had to make it to have eternal life.

Precious one, you do too. Most of the Pharisees rejected Jesus' words. They probably said something like, "That's a difficult statement. We can't follow You anymore." Why? Because they wanted life on their terms, and they couldn't have it that way. And neither can you. You get eternal life one way—His way. Jesus is the way, the truth, and the life, and this is the only way and truth and life, eternal life.

Now listen. Eternal life is not receiving communion. You can eat that bread and drink that wine all your life and not have eternal life. It's just bread and wine. You ask, "The bread and wine are not the body and flesh of Jesus Christ?" No, my friend, they aren't! The Word refers to one sacrifice for all time, and this sacrifice alone perfects forever those being sanctified (Hebrews 10:14). Jesus calls you to receive His words as truth. That's eating the flesh and drinking the blood of life—accepting Him and abiding in His Word. That's eternal life.

Many of Jesus' followers walked away, so Jesus turned to the twelve and asked, "You do not want to go away also, do you?" And they said, "Lord, to whom shall we go? You have the words of eternal life" (John 6:67-68).

These are words of life. Will you believe them? The work of God is to believe what Jesus said (John 6:29). Believe and receive; then you have life, my friend. You can be assured that you'll be raised up on that last day.

Who Is Your Father?

Do you realize that if Jesus Christ is not living in you by the power of His Holy Spirit, then your father is the devil? And do you realize that the devil is out to destroy you? What are you going to do? There's hope!

DAY ONE

Read John 7 before you begin any part of the assignment. Carefully note what's happening, where, and when. Don't forget to mark locations and references to time as you read. (Remember to mark the feasts because they help you understand the sequence of events throughout the book.)

Now, write out your insights in your notebook. What is happening in John 7? Where and when?

As you read through John 7 again, mark the following key words with their synonyms, pronouns, and various forms: *feast, believe, sign.*[10]

Also mark *the Christ*[11] in a special way. Make an exception this time, however: Do not mark other synonyms because all we want you to see in this chapter is the use of the term "the Christ." (By the way, *Christ* is the Greek term for the Hebrew *Messiah,* which means the "Anointed One"

51

God promised to send, who would deliver the Jews from their enemies and reign as their King.)

DAY TWO

Today read John 7 paragraph by paragraph. Remember, paragraphs group sentences together by subject (by theme, by thought, or by event).

As you finish each paragraph, summarize it in your notebook in a sentence or two. Watch for timing in each paragraph.

Here are the paragraph divisions in the NASB: John 7:1-9,10-13,14-18,19-24,25-31,32-36,37-39,40-44,45-53.

Now list everything you learned from marking *the Christ*.

Who were Jesus' enemies? Who hated Him and wanted to seize and kill Him? What do you learn from this?

Are you thirsty, my friend? Have you found anything to satisfy the deep emptiness and longing within? If you have one, has your religion satisfied you? Have you ever considered going to Jesus directly?

What do John 6:37,39,44, and 54 promise?

Finally, determine a theme for John 7 and record it on JOHN AT A GLANCE in the appendix.

DAY THREE

Read John 8 and mark *sin* distinctively. (Be sure to add this word to your bookmark.)

Now list in your notebook everything you learned in John 8 about sin.

Read through the chapter again and look for time indicators and locations. Mark these the same way you did in John 1–7.

DAY FOUR

Read John 8:1-11. In several sentences, summarize what this paragraph is about.

Leviticus 20:10-16 defines sexual sins. Read this passage and note various types of sexual misconduct and their penalties.

According to what you saw in Leviticus 20:10-16, why do you think the men brought the adulterous woman to Jesus?

How many does it take to commit adultery? Where was the man? Does this imply anything about the hearts and intents of these men?

How did Jesus handle the men? What did He want them to see?

How did Jesus respond to the woman? Did He approve her actions?

Are you living a sexually pure life or breaking God's law recorded in Leviticus 20? In light of what you've learned from marking the word *sin* throughout John 8, what would Jesus say to you or to anyone living immorally?

DAY FIVE

Read John 8:12-32 and mark the key words you have been marking throughout the Gospel of John if they are used in these verses. Also mark *true*[12] and *truth*.

When you observe the text, it's important to mark not only key words, geographical locations, and references to time, but also contrasts and comparisons. Contrasts and comparisons help us see in deeper, vivid, more picturesque ways what authors want their readers to understand.

Comparisons show how things are alike. (Many times an author will use "like" or "as" to introduce comparisons.) Look at John 8:12. What does Jesus compare Himself to in this verse?

Contrasts show how things are different or opposite—like sons of night and sons of day, light and darkness, the proud and the humble. Look again at John 8:12. What does Jesus contrast with those who follow Him?

Now read John 8:21-23. To whom is Jesus speaking? What does He contrast in these verses?

DAY SIX

According to John 8:24, why will some Jews die in their sins? What did they reject?

If you're using the New American Standard Bible, you'll notice the word *He* in verse 24 is italicized. (Italicized words were added by translators to make texts easier to understand.)

When Jesus said to the Jews, "Unless you believe that I am, you'll die in your sins," they asked Him who He was. Jesus had used the name God used to describe Himself to Moses (see Exodus 3:14-15). (We'll see this more clearly when we come to verse 58.)

When we speak of the deity of Jesus Christ, we're saying that Jesus is one with the Father, equal to Him in character and attributes.

Look at John 1:1-2,14. How do these verses show the deity of Jesus Christ?

The Gospel of John stresses the fact that Jesus Christ is not *a* god, but God in the flesh. As you study John, watch for other verses that show Jesus is one with the Father, God in the flesh.

What do you learn from the verses where Jesus calls Himself "I am" (John 8:24,28,58)?

The Jews stoned people for blasphemy. And Jesus' claim to be equal to the Father was certainly blasphemy from their perspective. We see this truth in verse 59 and in 10:33.

According to John 8:31-32, what do true disciples of Jesus do? Where is truth found?

What's contrasted in John 8:32-36?

In John 8:37-47, two fathers are contrasted. In your notebook, list what you learn about each and those who belong to them.

From what you just observed in God's Word, who is your father, and why do you say so?

Although Jesus Christ is God in the flesh, what kind of relationship did He have with the Father? Read through John 8:26-59 and list in your notebook everything you see about His relationship to the Father.

In other words, what the Father is, the Son is. What God does, Jesus does. This is true because Jesus shares His Father's nature—which is deity! Jesus is not just a man; He's the unique and permanent God-man from His incarnation.

Now, think about what you've written. Jesus demonstrates the way you should live in relationship to God the Father.

Now Beloved, we leave you with a few vital questions:

- ∞ Do you believe Jesus Christ is I AM (God)?

- ∞ According to God's Word in John 8:24, what happens to those who tell you Jesus Christ is not God in the flesh—that He's just *a* god, or prophet, or good man?

∽ Are Jesus' words true? What did He say? Are you going to believe God or man?

∽ If a man doesn't believe Jesus Christ and is not born again, who is his father? And what is his father like? (Look at John 8:44.)

Finally, determine a theme for John 8 and record it on JOHN AT A GLANCE in the appendix.

DAY SEVEN

  Store in your heart: John 8:44
Read and discuss: John 7:37-39; 8:12-59

QUESTIONS FOR DISCUSSION OR INDIVIDUAL STUDY

∽ Discuss your insights about the Spirit from John 7:37-39. (Who was the Spirit given to? When? How is He described?)

∽ What did the Jews mean about Jesus testifying about Himself? Was He?

∽ How does this lead into the discussion about fathers? Who is Jesus' Father?

∽ Who did the Jews claim for their father?

∽ Who did Jesus say the Jews' *true* father was and why?

- ∽ Discuss what you learned about the devil.

- ∽ What did Jesus mean when He said, "I am"? How did this relate to Abraham?

- ∽ What applications can you make in your own life? Who is your father, and why do you say this?

THOUGHT FOR THE WEEK

Does God care about you? Does He know about you—your circumstances, your background, your hurts, your struggles? Yes, He does know about you and care about you, Beloved. And He knows this, precious one: He knows whether you know Him, whether you believe His Son, the Lord Jesus Christ, is God in the flesh, and whether you're going to die in your sins. All who don't believe, who do not know God, whose father is the devil, will die in their sins. That's why Jesus Christ came. If you believe, the Father drew you to Him. He brought you to the fountain of living waters to drink fully of the blessed Holy Spirit.

You're not saved through faith in what God did in someone else. You're saved through faith in Jesus Christ as your Lord. The Lord may be working in others, but He wants to work in you. So don't worry if others don't believe; just examine yourself and make sure that *you* are walking the way you're supposed to walk.

When Jesus went up to celebrate the feast in Jerusalem, people were having all sorts of debates about Him. Jewish leaders repeatedly tried to seize and kill Him. Some Jews asked, "Isn't this the Christ?" Others answered, "No, we don't know where the Messiah comes from!"

The Jews had studied the Scriptures, but they didn't recognize that Jesus was the Christ. As a matter of fact, Jesus said, "You search the Scriptures…it is these that testify about Me; and you are unwilling to come to Me so that you may have life" (John 5:39-40). And most didn't go to Him. Why didn't they believe? Because they wanted to live the way *they* wanted to live, taking God on *their* terms. And you can't do that. God is God. He does not change—you're the one that has to change, confessing to Him something like this: *What I believed was wrong. I'm changing my mind* [repenting] *and coming to You.*

Jesus Christ always causes division. On that last day of the feast and during the final celebration, the priest poured out water, and the people sang and recited portions of the Old Testament, perhaps like this from Isaiah: "Everyone who thirsts, come to the waters; and you who have no money, come, buy and eat" (Isaiah 55:1). This time, Jesus said, "If anyone is thirsty, let him come to Me and drink." The Greek tense can be translated "Let him keep on coming to Me. Let him keep on drinking of Me. He who believes in Me…from his innermost being will flow rivers of living water." John comments, "But this He spoke of the Spirit, whom those who believed in Him were to receive; for the Spirit was not yet given, because Jesus was not yet glorified" (John 7:37-39).

Now Jesus teaches the religious leaders who reject Him that their father is the devil (8:44) and that they do his works (8:41). Do you know people who think they belong to God but don't?

The Father sent Jesus Christ to give life to the world, but the devil's purpose is to kill and destroy. He's a thief. He's a liar. He's a murderer. He's the father of lies, and he does not abide in the truth. He wants to destroy you. He can and does deceive people who think they are Christians—who have a religion but not a relationship with God. There's no life in the devil, only death. Jesus is the only one who has eternal life to give.

And Jesus does satisfy. My friend, I don't know what you're seeking, but I can tell you that eternal life is available in the One who said, "If anyone is thirsty, let him come to me and drink." He'll satisfy you, and the devil will no longer be your father. Remember that Jesus did not come into the world to condemn you. He didn't have to because you were condemned already. And if He didn't come to save you, you would stay condemned, your father would continue to be the devil, you would die and go to hell, you would be resurrected to stand before God, and you would be cast into the lake of fire where the worm does not die and the fire is not quenched. Every human being born of flesh into this world is going to live forever—either in the presence of God or in the presence of the devil. The only way you can escape hell and the lake of fire is to know Jesus Christ. That's why He stood on that great day of the feast and cried out to that multitude.

When He was calling these people to come and drink of Him, He was identifying Himself with the water the priests were pouring out, reminding the people that the water symbolizes something else. When you come to Jesus, you drink Him in—the Spirit creates living waters inside you, you're set free from sin, and you're delivered from the domain of darkness into the very kingdom of God. God replaces the devil as your father.

The next day, Jesus continued, "'I am the Light of the world; he who follows Me will not walk in the darkness, but will have the Light of life'" (8:12). The Pharisees accuse Him for bearing witness to Himself. Now we saw in chapter 5 that the full witness to Jesus included the Father, John the Baptist, Jesus' own works, and the Scriptures—including the testimony of Moses, whom the Pharisees held so sacred.

So Jesus responds, "Even if I testify about Myself, my witness is true, for I know where I came from and where I am going; but you do not know where I come from or where I am going. You judge according to the flesh; I am not judging anyone. But even if I do judge, My judgment is true; for I am not alone in it, but I and the Father who sent Me" (8:14-16). Then He says, "I go away, and you will seek Me, and you will die in your sin; where I am going, you cannot come" (verse 21).

The Jews imagined He was going to kill Himself. But Jesus responded, "You are from below, I am from above; you are of this world, I am not of this world." This radical contrast is consistent with the radical contrast between the two fathers.

Then Jesus says one of the most important things for us to know from John: "Unless you believe that I am [the "He" is added, as we pointed out], you will die in your sins." They don't know what He's saying, so they ask, "Who are You?" Then Jesus answers, "What have I been saying to you from the beginning? I have many things to speak and to judge concerning you, but He who sent Me is true; and the things which I heard from Him, these I speak to the world."

What was wrong with these people? They had religion without relationship. They were walking in darkness. If they had the Light of life, they would have followed the Lord Jesus Christ. Why were they walking in darkness? Because they were of their father the devil—the murderer, liar, and destroyer. Jesus explains further:

"He who sent Me is with Me; He has not left Me alone, for I always do the things that are pleasing to Him." As He spoke these things, many came to believe in Him. So Jesus was saying to those Jews who had believed in Him, "If you continue in My word, then you are truly disciples of Mine; and you will know the truth, and the truth will make you free."

They answered Him, "We are Abraham's descendants and have never yet been enslaved to anyone; how is it that You say, 'You will become free'?"

Jesus answered them, "Truly, truly, I say to you, everyone who commits sin is the slave of sin. The slave does not remain in the house forever; the son does remain forever. So if the Son makes you free, you will be free indeed. I know that you are Abraham's descendants; yet you seek to kill Me, because My word has no place in you" (8:29-37).

Then Jesus adds, "I speak the things which I have seen with My Father; therefore you also do the things which you heard from your father." Now here's the contrast: "They answered and said to Him, 'Abraham is our father.' Jesus said to them, 'If you are Abraham's children, do the deeds of Abraham.'" Now what did Abraham do? He looked forward in faith and believed in God's promise.

Jesus says (in effect), "All right, you have a father. And your father is not the same as My Father. You're doing the deeds of *your* father, not the *true* Father." Now watch what He goes on to say.

"But as it is, you are seeking to kill Me, a man who has told you the truth, which I heard from God; this Abraham did not do. You are doing the deeds of your father."

They said to Him, "We were not born of fornication; we have one Father: God."

Jesus said to them, "If God were your Father, you would love Me, for I proceeded forth and have come from God, for I have not even come on My own initiative, but He sent Me. Why do you not understand what I am saying? It is because you cannot hear My Word. You are of your father the devil, and you want to do the desires of your father. He was a murderer from the beginning, and does not stand in the truth because there is no truth in him. Whenever he speaks a lie, he speaks from his own nature; for he is a liar and the father of lies. But because I speak the truth, you do not believe Me" (8:40-45).

Now Jesus is truth. The Father is truth. The Father sent the Son that we might have life and that we might have it abundantly and eternally.

God sent His Son to this world to speak truth. Do you believe Him? If you do, you have been set free. If you don't, you're listening to the liar, the murderer, the destroyer, and you will share his destiny. How different this Jesus is who went to Calvary to take your punishment so you wouldn't have to bear it. If the devil sacrifices time and effort, he does it only to destroy you, not to save you. He wants to do this because he's malevolent. He wishes your worst. But the benevolent God wishes your best. He loved you and sent His Son so that you might be set free.

I want you to know, precious one, that you have a father. Your father is either God or the devil. If you receive Jesus Christ, you'll have the most wonderful Father, far beyond your expectations.

You say, "How does God reach people far away, who don't have this message?" God can reach anybody, but He wants you to know now that He's a Father who loves you and cares for you. Won't you believe?

RUNNING YOUR OWN
LIFE OR OBEYING GOD?

Have you ever wondered, my friend, why your life isn't doing any better than it is? Maybe it's because you're your own god—you're running your own life.

DAY ONE

Read John 9 today, marking the following key words: *sign, sin, blind, believe, see (sight)*. Mark *see* with two eyes like this: ◉◉. Mark *blind* by shading the eyes brown or drawing a slash through the eyes like this ◉◉. (These are just some ideas—choose your own marking if you like.) Also watch for and mark time indicators and locations.

List what you learned from marking these key words.

DAY TWO

What is John 9 about? Who are the main characters? Where do events take place? When—what day of the week?

Compare the main characters by listing what you learn about them in columns:

Jesus   The blind man   His parents   The Jews

Finally, determine a theme for John 9 and record it on JOHN AT A GLANCE.

DAY THREE

Read John 10 and mark references to *sheep* including pronouns (*them* or *they*). Mark *flock* the same way.
Watch for and mark *blind* as you did in chapter 9.

DAY FOUR

Read John 10 again. Mark time indicators and locations. Also mark the following key words and their pronouns: *shepherd, the Jews, believe, sign, the door, the thief,* and *the Christ*. Mark *the shepherd* the same way you marked *Jesus* all along, but mark *the Christ* the way you marked it in chapter 7. We've seen that *Christ* (Greek) and *Messiah* (Hebrew) refer to the one who comes to deliver the Jews and rule as King. Remember that John was writing because he wanted us to know and believe that Jesus was the Christ.

Make a list of everything you learn about the Shepherd and the sheep.

Also list what you learn about the thief. Whom is the thief contrasted with? List the ways they differ.

If Jesus is the Shepherd, whom do you think the thief represents? Compare the characteristics of the thief with the one mentioned in John 8:44.

DAY FIVE

When you read a chapter that contains a particular teaching, such as John 10 presents sheep and the Shepherd, always try to find out what prompts the teaching. Think about what happened in John 9 and how that relates to the teaching in John 10. Also remember what you saw when you marked *blind* in chapter 10 because Jesus and those around Him were discussing what happened in John 9. What was the occasion? Jesus is a master Teacher—He uses occasions to teach valuable lessons.

Did the Pharisees (Jews) want to go to heaven?

Were they willing to go through a door if the door was Jesus?

What did the Jews accuse Jesus of in John 10:33?

Were the Jews blind to who Jesus was? Were they sheep from His sheepfold?

DAY SIX

Review John 20:30-31, which gives John's purpose for writing this Gospel.

How does John 9–10 help John accomplish this purpose?

In case you missed it, read John 10:30-39 again. How do these verses show the deity of Jesus Christ (the fact that

Jesus is God in the flesh, one with the Father in character and attributes, such as holiness, righteousness, mercy, and love)?

When you study your Bible, be sure to write down cross-references in the margin. Cross-references are other verses that teach the same thing or help you understand more clearly what you're studying. The deity of Jesus Christ is important, so set up a system of cross-references where this teaching is mentioned. For example, if you want to cross-reference this subject in John, you can write "Deity" in the margin next to John 1:1 and then put the next reference that supports the deity of Christ underneath, like this:

Deity
John 1:14

Then, in the margin of John 1:14, write "Deity" along with the next reference, and so on.

Now review what you observed and listed about the sheep and the Shepherd on day four. At the end of today's lesson is a section called Insights on Sheep. You'll enjoy reading these! They are fascinating—describing what many people are like today! They will help you appreciate what Jesus says in John 10. (Remember, the Jews of Jesus' day were far more familiar with sheep than most of us are today.)

After you read this article, make a list of the ways you relate to what you learned. In what ways are you like a sheep?

According to what you learned from John 10, what's the only way to get into God's sheepfold? What will happen to God's sheep? Is Jesus Christ your Shepherd, or would you like to have Him as your Shepherd? Would you like to be His sheep?

Record a theme for John 10 on JOHN AT A GLANCE.

INSIGHTS ON SHEEP

1. The life of a sheep depends a lot on what kind of shepherd it has. If the sheep has a mean or cruel shepherd, it would probably suffer, and its life would be hard. Or if the shepherd were lazy and didn't take care of the sheep, it might be hungry or even starve!

    But if the shepherd was gentle and brave and didn't think of himself first, then the sheep would grow to be healthy, strong, content, and happy.

2. More than any other kind of animal, sheep need attention and care. The shepherd must protect the sheep from cougars, wolves, dogs, and thieves. The shepherd must protect his sheep *at all times* of the day and night. (And you know, God is your Shepherd, and He protects you all the time too!)

3. Sheep are timid and fearful animals. They get scared very easily, and this fear keeps them from doing many things that are good for them.

4. Sheep are "mass-minded"—they have "mob instincts"—they will all do what every other sheep is doing! If one sheep gets scared and runs, all the others will run with it, whether or not they know why they are running.

5. Sheep are animals of habit. They like to keep following the same trails over and over. They will keep grazing on the same land until they practically ruin the land—and they will eat bad grass!

6. Sheep are also known to be very stubborn animals. They need the shepherd to guide them around.

7. Sheep are very stupid, dumb animals. They will sometimes just freeze if there is danger around. Sometimes they won't even try to run to safety; they will panic and not even cry out.

8. It's easy to tell who owns the sheep because each shepherd gives his sheep an earmark. The earmark is like a brand mark. The shepherd cuts a certain mark into each one of the sheep's ears. And each shepherd gives all his sheep the same earmark.

9. Sheep will not lie down and rest unless they...
   a. are not afraid
   b. get along with all the other sheep
   c. do not have any flies or pests bothering them
   d. are not hungry

10. Sheep will butt each other with their heads. They also have a "butting order." The oldest sheep usually has the highest position of power. If a younger sheep is eating in a patch of grass the oldest one wants, he will butt the younger one out of the way! The younger ones will act just the same way to sheep younger than themselves. But when the shepherd comes around, the sheep forget what they were fighting over, and they stop and behave themselves.

11. A sheep has to have good land to feed on, or it will stay hungry! If a sheep is hungry, it will stay on its feet and constantly be searching for food to satisfy its hunger. Sheep cannot sleep

if they are hungry, and they are not much good to the owner if they stay in that condition. They get nervous and upset very easily, and if they don't eat the right food, all sorts of things will bother them.

12. Sheep are bothered by many different pests— all kinds of flies, mosquitoes, gnats, and other flying insects. Many of these insects will aim straight for the nose of the sheep! If they get in the sheep's nose, they may lay eggs. When the eggs hatch, the larvae will get into the passages of the nose and cause swelling and irritations and sometimes blindness. The sheep will beat their heads against trees or rocks to try to get these pests to stop bothering them, and sometimes this may kill the sheep. Other sheep will shake their heads for hours and hours. Some will run until they just drop from running so much. The first time a good shepherd sees this happening to his sheep, he puts oil on the sheep's head and around the nose. This will calm the sheep.

13. Sheep have to have water! A sheep's body is 70 percent water, so water has a lot to do with how healthy and strong a sheep stays. Sheep get their water mainly from three places:

    a. springs and streams
    b. deep wells
    c. dew on the grass (yes, dew on the grass!)

    Sheep can go for long periods of time if they can get the dew off the grass early in the morning before the sun evaporates it.

14. Sheep can become "cast down." This means that they get turned over on their back and cannot

get up again by themselves. If the shepherd doesn't come to the sheep quickly, the sheep may die! Once the shepherd finds a sheep in this position, he speaks to it gently and rubs its legs to get its circulation going again. A sheep becomes "cast down" because it's looking for a soft spot, because it  has too much wool, or because it's just too fat!

15. In the sheepfold—the place where the sheep sleep—the shepherd lies down in the opening or doorway to guard the sheep. If thieves or predators try to get in and hurt the sheep, they have to cross over the shepherd—because he's the door.*

DAY SEVEN

Store in your heart: John 10:27-28
Read and discuss: John 9:1-11,35-41; 10:1-18,25-30

QUESTIONS FOR DISCUSSION OR INDIVIDUAL STUDY

ᘉ Discuss the sign recorded in John 9. Be sure to cover what you learn about the hearts of the blind man and the Jews and their attitude about Jesus.

---

* The information in INSIGHTS ON SHEEP was gathered from Phillip Keller, *A Shepherd Looks at Psalm 23* (Grand Rapids, MI: Zondervan Publishing House, 1988). Used by permission.

∾ Discuss the Shepherd, the sheep, and the thief from chapter 10.

∾ Why did Jesus use this figure of speech?

∾ How did the Pharisees react to Jesus' use of this figure of speech?

∾ Talk about who receives eternal life, how long they keep it, and if anyone can take it away.

∾ Do the Shepherd's true sheep live differently from those who do not belong to Him?

∾ Discuss how chapter 10 relates to chapter 9.

THOUGHT FOR THE WEEK

In chapter 9, a man who was blind from birth was first healed by Jesus Christ and then kicked out of a synagogue. But he tells his Pharisee accusers he knows one thing—that he was blind but now sees. He reminds them that no man has ever healed a blind person, that God doesn't hear sinners, and that a man named Jesus opened his blind eyes.

When Jesus asks him if he believes in the Son of Man, he asks, "Who is He, Lord, that I may believe in Him?" When Jesus tells him, he says, "Lord, I believe." His faith cost him something. Believing will cost you something too, but not believing will cost you far more. After this man received his sight, he learned that Jesus was the anointed Son of Man—the Son of God. From that point on, God was going to run his life.

This ties in with Jesus' figure of speech about a shepherd and his sheepfold (chapter 10). The Pharisees kicked the man out of their fold, but Jesus took him into His own—the only fold that's going to count. He is the true door to the true sheepfold, and all other doors (who are hired hands, not owners) leave the sheep vulnerable to wolves. Jesus wants us to know He's the door, the Good Shepherd of the sheep.

Which door have you gone through? Are you being led by a hired hand, vulnerable to attack by wolves or thieves who come only to steal, kill, and destroy? Or are you being led safely by the Lord Jesus Christ? Well, you have two paths to choose from. One is God's path, which is straight and narrow, through Jesus, who is the way, the truth, and the life. The other is the crooked and broad path that leads to the wolf's stomach—to death and destruction.

Right after this we see Jesus walking in the temple in the portico of Solomon during the Feast of Dedication (in the winter). The Jews ask Him how long He plans to keep them in suspense by not stating plainly whether He's the Messiah. Jesus says He has already told them but that they don't want to believe. He repeats that the works He has done in His Father's name bear witness to who He is. Now watch what He says: "But you do not believe because you are not of My sheep."

Now remember, Jesus said no one comes to Him unless the Father draws him (chapter 6). Now He adds, "My sheep hear My voice, and I know them, and they follow Me; and I give eternal life to them, and they will never perish; and no one will snatch them out of My hand."

This is blessed assurance. If you're His sheep, no one ever will separate you from Him. But remember that if you are His sheep, you follow Him. He doesn't say His sheep *should* follow Him; He says they *do*. All sheep are followers; the rest are goats (Matthew 25).

All of this is happening at the Feast of Dedication during the winter. You say, "Wait a minute! I don't see a Feast of Dedication on my chart!" That's because the Jews, not God, inaugurated the Feast of Dedication. God ordained the Feasts of Passover, Pentecost, and Tabernacles (or Booths, which Jesus celebrated, according to chapter 7). These are recorded in the book of Leviticus.

The Feast of Dedication is also called the Festival of Lights and Hanukkah. According to the Talmud, it commemorates the miracle of one day's supply of olive oil burning for eight days in a lamp when the Jews were cleansing and rededicating the temple after the Greek Seleucids desecrated it around 165 BC. The feast usually occurs in our December, but it can start as early as late November and end as late as early January.

While the Jews are celebrating this festival of lights, remembering a light that lasted eight days, they don't realize that the eternal Light of the world stands before them. The Shekinah glory that departed from the temple just before the Babylonian captivity is standing in their presence. The Shekinah glory is the presence of God, which led them out of the wilderness, across the Red Sea, and to Mount Sinai. It hovered over the tabernacle for 40 years in the wilderness and filled Solomon's temple. This presence of God departed from the temple during Ezekiel's ministry because of Israel's and Judah's sin. Now that Shekinah glory in the person of Jesus Christ stands before them. But they are blind; they cannot see the light. And if you have not yet seen that Jesus Christ is God in the flesh, you too are blind, and John 8:24 says you will die in your sins.

The deity of Jesus Christ is the line between life and death, heaven and hell. It stands between an eternity with no more sorrow, tears, death, and pain, and an eternity in the lake of fire. The line is what you believe about this man called Jesus. Will you believe He's the God-man? The Jews had trouble with this. John 10:27 says, "My sheep hear My voice," and His voice declares His deity. He says, "I know them, and they follow Me; and I give eternal life to them, and they will never perish; and no one will snatch them out of My hand." Why? Because "My Father...has given them to Me" and "I and the Father are one" (10:29-30).

The Jews took up stones again to stone Him. When Jesus asked which good work they were stoning Him for, they answered, "For a good work we do not stone You, but for blasphemy; and because You, being a man, make Yourself out to be God." They understood that Jesus Christ was identifying His saving hand with His Father's, making Himself equal in sovereignty to God, and so they were going to stone Him. These Jews knew that Leviticus 24:10-16 clearly commands the death penalty for blasphemy.

Some people will say, "But Jesus never claimed to be God. He claimed to be a god." If you have your Bible marked with the cross-references to the deity of Jesus, you can show from God's Word that He is God. And when the Jews talked about equality with God, they had in mind the one God of Israel, no other god, which would be idolatry to them. Throughout the centuries, many of them feared blaspheming so much they not only avoided pronouncing the personal name of God (the Tetragrammaton: YHWH), they even spelled His generic name like this: "G_d."

According to John 8:24, Jesus says, "Unless you believe that I am...you will die in your sins." We've talked about this "I Am" before—the name God revealed to Moses at the burning bush. When Jesus applied this name to Himself, He was using the great and fearful name of the Lord. The Jews knew what name He used and interpreted His claim to be "I Am" as blasphemy. They didn't recognize that Jesus truly *is* God. They were blinded to the radiance of God's glory and the exact representation of His nature (Hebrews 1:3).

Now I want to ask you a question. Whom are you going to believe, the people who knock on your door or the Son who said, "I Am"? Precious one, if you don't believe that Jesus Christ is God, you will die in your sins. You may be saying, "I don't want to die in my sins, but I'm not sure I can believe that He's God." Go to Him and ask; keep studying the Gospel of John and you'll see for yourself. When you receive Him, you'll have life in His name.

What Happens When You Die?

Someday, my friend, we're going to die. We don't like to talk about it; we prefer to avoid it, but we're going to die. Death is inevitable for every human being unless the Lord Jesus Christ comes first. But the question is, do you know what's going to happen to you when you die? Do you understand the process, and are you sure that what you know is based on pure, unadulterated truth—not the opinions, experiences, or feelings of other people, but on the Word of God? If you don't know what the Word of God says, you don't know truth, so that's what we're going to look at this week.

DAY ONE

Read John 11 today, marking geographical locations and looking them up on your map. Mark time indicators too. You'll need to go back to John 10:40 and make certain you marked that reference in order to understand where Jesus is in John 11:6.

Mark the following key words: *death, believe, life,* and *blind* (remember how you marked this in John 9 and 10).

DAY TWO

Read John 11 again. This time mark every reference to the following people: *Lazarus, Jesus, Mary, Martha,* and *the Christ.*

List everything you learned about Jesus and Lazarus from this chapter.

DAY THREE

Read John 11 again, and this time list everything you learn about Mary and Martha.

As we have said before, when you read the Word of God, be sure to compare Scripture with Scripture. To get more insight into Mary and Martha, read Luke 10:38-42.

Now, thinking about what you saw about Mary and Martha, answer these questions:

- ∾ Which woman are you more like? (Yes, men exhibit these traits too—they're not exclusively female.) Why?

- ∾ What can you apply to your own life from Luke 10:38-42?

DAY FOUR

What do you think happens to a person at death?

Where do your beliefs come from—what are they based on? Can you trust them? Why?

Let's take a few moments and see what the Word of God says happens when a person dies. Look up the following verses. As you read, remember these are from the Word of

God. Write in your notebook what you learn from these verses about people who believe on the Lord Jesus Christ and therefore have been born again:

> John 3:16
>
> John 5:21,24
>
> John 6:37,39,44
>
> John 8:51

DAY FIVE

Today we'll continue looking at what the Word of God says happens at death. Read the following verses, and as you did yesterday, write in your notebook what you learn about people who have believed on the Lord Jesus Christ and therefore are born again.

> Philippians 1:21-23
>
> John 14:1-3
>
> 2 Corinthians 5:8
>
> Revelation 21:3-6

Now, how do these words from God compare with your beliefs or what you've been taught?

Lastly, list all you learn from marking *believe* in John 11.

DAY SIX

Today we want to look at what happens to those who do *not* believe Jesus is the Christ, the Son of God, and therefore do not have life in His name. Read the following passages and record in your notebook what you learn about those who don't believe.

John 3:36

John 5:28-29

John 8:24

Revelation 20:11-15

Revelation 21:8

Has this been an eye-opener for you? You've just looked at what God says about those who don't believe. Summarize what you learned.

Review what you learned from marking *believe* in John 11. Now, beloved one for whom Christ died, have you truly believed? Do your deeds—the way you live, you act, you treat people, you obey God's Word—show that you believe?

Isn't this awesome? Jesus loved you and died for you when you were a sinner. He doesn't ask you to change yourself, to clean yourself up first; He takes you just the way you are. However, when you come to Him, believing He is God and the Lamb of God who takes away your sins, He becomes your Shepherd and gives you eternal life. You will never perish—no one will ever take you out of God's hand. And He will raise you up, and you will live with Him forever and ever.

DAY SEVEN

 Store in your heart: John 11:25
Read and discuss: John 11:1-45

QUESTIONS FOR DISCUSSION OR INDIVIDUAL STUDY

- ∾ What miraculous sign did Jesus perform in John 11, and why is it so important? What does it show about Jesus?

- ∾ How did Jesus respond to the news of Lazarus' death? What did He know?

- ∾ How did different characters in the chapter react to Jesus' actions?

- ∾ Discuss what Mary and Martha did when Jesus arrived. How do they compare and contrast with each other?

- ∾ Are you more similar to Mary or to Martha?

- ∾ According to the Scriptures, what happens to believers at death?

- ∾ What happens to unbelievers when they die?

- ∾ How do these teachings compare to what you've heard from others? Which is true? Do you need to make any changes?

THOUGHT FOR THE WEEK

Of all the things men fear, none is greater than death. Why? Because without revelation from God, death is a mystery. And to the majority of people it means the end—nonexistence.

Lazarus was sick, and his sisters asked Jesus to come. He responded to the news by saying, "This sickness is not to end in death, but for the glory of God, that the Son of God may be glorified by it." Though Jesus doesn't go immediately, He does let His disciples know that Lazarus will be all right when He says, "Our friend Lazarus has fallen asleep; but I go, that I may awaken him out of sleep." Remember that Jesus loved Lazarus, and Lazarus loved Him and believed in Him. So death to the Christian is not the end that most understand it to be. When Jesus said Lazarus had fallen asleep, the disciples were confused: "Lord, if he has fallen asleep, he will recover." Jesus spoke of death, but they thought He was speaking of literal sleep. So Jesus said to them plainly, "Lazarus is dead, and I am glad for your sakes that I was not there, so that you may believe."

Jesus had already healed blind and paralyzed people. But raising the dead showed quite another dimension because this was an even clearer demonstration of God's power. When Jesus raised Lazarus, He showed His divine power and authority. This became the sign of signs—until He raised Himself from the dead (John 2:19; 10:18).

When Jesus came to Bethany (about two miles from Jerusalem), He found that Lazarus had been in his tomb for four days. Some Jews came to Martha and Mary to console them concerning their brother. But the sisters had heard that Jesus was coming, and as He approached, Martha took off to meet Him. Mary waited until Jesus asked her to come. Martha said to Jesus, "Lord, if You had been here, my brother would not have died." This is not an accusation but a confession of faith in His power to heal. Martha believed Jesus was the Christ, the Son of God. She adds, "Even now I know that whatever You ask of God, God will give You." Jesus answered, "Your brother will rise again."

Martha didn't expect Lazarus to come back to life. This is clear from her next words: "I know that he will rise again in the resurrection on the last day." Then Jesus said to her, "I am the resurrection and the life." Remember what John said in the beginning: "In Him was life, and the life was the

Light of men." Then Jesus added, "He who believes in Me will live even if he dies."

So you can know this: Death is inevitable, but it's not the end if you know Jesus. You're going to live. Lazarus died, but his condition was not permanent—Jesus called the experience "sleep." You fall asleep and wake up in the presence of God. Revelation 20:5 says, "The rest of the dead did not come to life until the thousand years were completed. This is the first resurrection" (the raising of believers). Then the Word says, "Blessed and holy is the one who has a part in the first resurrection; over these the second death has no power, but they will be priests of God and of Christ and will reign with Him for a thousand years."

Now what is this "second death"? When you and I are born the first time, we're born of flesh, born dead in trespasses and sins. We're born in a state of sin, and the wages of sin is death. If we come to know the Lord Jesus Christ and are born *again,* we don't experience this second death, which Revelation 20:14 says is "the lake of fire." So when Jesus says you'll never die, He is referring to the separation from God in the lake of fire. Those who are born again spend all eternity with Him.

In John 11:27, Martha tells Jesus she believes that He is "the Christ, the Son of God, even He who comes into the world." When Mary arrives, she falls at His feet, saying, "Lord, if You had been here, my brother would not have died." Jesus was deeply moved by this expression of faith. At the same time, He was probably angry with the one who brought death into the world through deceit and seduction. In the Garden of Eden, he murdered (John 8:44) mankind, which was in the loins of Adam. All men descended from Adam and Eve (the mother of all living) and became subject to sin and death. Death was Jesus' enemy, but He conquered it as the resurrection and the life, and you can be victorious in Him as well.

What happens when a person dies? Well, we saw Jesus deeply moved in His spirit at the presence of death. Why? Because death is what He came to abolish. Death kept men from God and from eternal life. When we see Him weeping (John 11:35), we see human passion. Jesus is touched by our weaknesses, grieving in His heart and shedding tears. This is God in flesh, weeping over our pain.

In 1 Corinthians 15 (the resurrection chapter), Paul says the last enemy conquered is death, and Jesus is the conqueror. He won't lose *one* of His own. Those who die apart from Christ go to the lake of fire. They'll live forever in a place where their worm does not die, and the fire is not quenched (Mark 9:44,46,48). But you can know this, precious one: No one goes to this place for lack of opportunity—it belongs to those who reject Christ their entire lives. God doesn't lose any of His own. As you study the Scriptures, you'll see this for yourself.

Lazarus was in the tomb four days. By the fourth day, everyone knew he had been dead long enough to smell bad. But Jesus said to Martha, "Did I not say to you that if you believe, you will see the glory of God?" Now "glory" means valuation, so here Jesus says they'll see what God is really like. You're going to see who Jesus really is—the resurrection and the life. So they remove the stone, and Jesus raises His eyes and thanks God for hearing Him in advance so that those standing by might believe. Now remember how John closes his Gospel: The signs he includes are written so that unbelievers might come to faith in the Son of God and have life in His name. "And when He had said these things, He cried out with a loud voice, 'Lazarus, come forth.' The man who had died came forth."

I want to make sure you understand where you're headed if you know Christ and where you'll go if you don't because you *are* going to die. If Jesus returns while you're alive and you believe in Him, you'll ascend to meet Him in the air with other believers, alive and dead. If not, you'll be left behind. You need to know this now.

Those who die not knowing the Son of God go to a place called *Hades* in Greek and *Sheol* in Hebrew. Luke 16:28 describes it as a "place of torment." No one who goes there can escape that torment. People don't believe it exists, and even if someone did come back from the dead to testify, people who reject Moses (the Law) and the prophets still wouldn't believe it (Luke 16:31). Hades is separated from a place of comfort (the bosom of Abraham) by an uncrossable chasm.

Today, the testimonies circulating about people being raised from the dead have nothing to do with salvation. The object of faith should not be other people's experiences but rather the Lord Jesus Christ and His work.

I believe that after Jesus died, the believers in the place of comfort were caught up into heaven, and the comfortable part of Sheol, the bosom of Abraham, was emptied. So those who looked forward to the coming of the Lord in the Old Testament went to heaven. All that remains of Sheol is the place of torment, Hades. The Bible says that hell enlarges itself (Isaiah 5:14), meaning it continues to receive men in big numbers, in agreement with Jesus' teaching that the path to destruction is broad. If you don't know the Lord Jesus Christ when you die, you're going to go to this place.

There you'll stay until Jesus returns to earth and sets up His kingdom. After He rules on earth for a thousand years (Revelation 20:1-7), Sheol itself empties the dead that are in it to face the Great White Throne judgment, where they're judged according to their deeds. Why? Because they refused God's grace and forgiveness. They refused to believe what the Lord did for sinners.

Then they're going to be cast into the lake of fire, where "their worm does not die, and the fire is not quenched." Isaiah says believers will go and look on the corpses of the men who transgressed against God (66:24). Those who do not believe will be in torment forever and ever. You say, "I thought you said I was going to die." Yes, you're going to die the second death. And that second death is the lake of fire (Revelation 20:14).

What about the person who receives the Lord Jesus Christ? Second Corinthians 5:1 says, "If the earthly tent which is our house is torn down, we have a building from God, a house not made with hands, eternal in the heavens." In other words, we're going to have a new body, as 1 Corinthians 15 also describes. Paul is saying that if this earthly body is torn down (dies), you have a brand-new body waiting for you. Verse 5 adds, "Now He who prepared us for this very purpose is God, who gave to us the Spirit as a pledge." The Spirit is a pledge of something to come. So right now while we're at home in the body, we're absent from the Lord. If we love the Lord and are intimate with Him, news of our impending death will be exciting. Why? Because death puts us in the presence of the Lord, from whom we're absent as long as we're in our bodies.

Soul sleep is a myth. The instant you die, you're absent from the body. That same instant, you're present with the Lord. So this we have as our ambition—to please the Lord whether we're at home with Him or absent.

So precious one, if you know Jesus Christ, the instant you die you're absent from the body and present with the Lord, right there with Jesus Christ by the throne of God.

The Bible teaches that when He returns to earth, He will descend from heaven with the sound of a trumpet and raise the dead in Christ. If you're dead, the body you left behind will be resurrected. If you're alive, your mortal body will immediately put on immortality. You will be caught up together with all those who believed in Jesus. We will meet the Lord together in the air and be with Him forever.

Is death our enemy? Yes it is, but God promises to conquer this enemy once for all time in the resurrection, when life swallows it up. Death is inevitable, my friend. How you face it will be determined by your relationship with Jesus Christ and your sure knowledge of the Word of God.

EXTRAVAGANT LOVE

Would you ever want extravagant love from someone you betrayed? Or would you think such a person was a fool? Suppose someone *does* love you with an extravagant love. Would you like to know who it is and why this person loves you so much in spite of your behavior?

DAY ONE

Read John 11:54-57 today. This passage contains important information about Jesus and His ministry. From the verses, record answers to the following questions in your notebook:

∾ What's going to change in Jesus' ministry? From whom is Jesus withdrawing?

∾ When is this happening? What feast is at hand? Look at your chart on THE FEASTS OF ISRAEL in the appendix and note when this feast is celebrated.

∾ Two groups of people are eager to see Jesus. Who are they, and what do they want to know?

Record a theme for John 11 on JOHN AT A GLANCE.

Now read John 12 paragraph by paragraph. Different versions and editions of the Bible start paragraphs in different ways: with verse numbers bolder than others, with space between paragraphs, or with the first line indented.

As you read through John 12, watch for and mark two things:

First, as you have done before, mark every reference to time and geographical locations. This will help you understand the chronological and geographical context of these events. When we talk about "chronological context," we mean the timing and order of events—how one event follows another. Remember to check the map in the appendix to locate sites mentioned. Also remember that if God tells us these things in His Word, He wants us to know them.

Second, note people Jesus comes in contact with and their responses to Him. Record in the margins of your Bible where Jesus is, what He's doing, and whom He is with. For example, at verse 1 you can write, "In Bethany with Lazarus, Mary, and Martha."

Then at verses 9-11 you might write, "Large crowd goes to see Jesus; priests plot Lazarus's death."

Doing an exercise like this, looking at a chapter paragraph by paragraph, helps you see everything the chapter records.

DAYS TWO & THREE

Read through John 12 again, marking the key words *king, sign*,[13] *hour, Son of Man, believe*,[14] *judge*,[15] *Light, eternal life*, and *world*. You may want to mark *king* with a gold crown and *judge* with a black gavel, color *Light* yellow, and draw a blue circle around *world*. Mark the rest according to your bookmark.

Make a list of everything you learn about the words you mark. Remember to ask the 5 W's and H: who, what, when, where, why, and how. Get answers directly from the verses—don't add your own thoughts; this way you know you're handling God's Word accurately. For example, ask who a certain king is, what he is king of, what is said about him, how he comes on the scene, and how he's recognized.

When you make your list about signs, note what they refer to and how people respond to them.

DAY FOUR

Read John 13. Carefully watch events in this chapter, noting what they are, where they take place, why they occur, and what they mean. Also note subjects (such as certain people and God) and why they're mentioned. Particularly observe what Jesus says in this chapter and to whom. Be sure to mark time indicators and locations as before and ask the 5 W's and H.

Mark all your key words and add *love* to your bookmark. We'll look for this word in several upcoming chapters.

DAY FIVE

Review the key words in John 13, write down some of your observations, and answer the following questions. Be brief and to the point in your answers.

- ∾ What is this chapter about?

- ∾ Who are the major characters, and what do you learn about them?

- ∾ Why did Jesus wash the disciples' feet? Did He wash the feet of all of them? Did He exclude Judas? (What was Judas going to do?) What does this tell you?

- ∾ When does the event described in John 13 take place? Why is it at that time?

- ∾ What truths and lessons does Jesus teach, and to whom do they apply?

DAY SIX

In John 12:23,27 and 13:1, Jesus refers to "the hour," "this hour," and "His hour." From observing the texts, what hour do you think Jesus is referring to?

Look up the following references and note what you learn about each use of the phrase "His [My] hour had [has] not yet come." Note when it's said and what's happening in each instance.

John 2:4

John 7:30

John 8:20

Now, in light of what you saw in John 12–13 about "the hour," what do you learn about the death of Jesus Christ? Was it planned or an accident? If planned, by whom?

According to John 12:23-27, why did Jesus come?

When we come to John 19, we'll study Jesus' crucifixion in greater detail. For now, look at John 12:32-33. Did Jesus know how He was going to die? Explain how you know from these verses.

Well, that's it for this week, Beloved! Don't forget to record themes for John 12 and 13 on JOHN AT A GLANCE in the appendix.

DAY SEVEN

 Store in your heart: John 13:34-35
Read and discuss: John 12:1-19,27-50; 13:1-35

QUESTIONS FOR DISCUSSION OR INDIVIDUAL STUDY

- ∞ What did you learn about Mary's devotion to Jesus and Judas' response?

- ∞ Do similar exchanges happen today?

- ∞ Discuss Jesus' entry to Jerusalem on a donkey and the people heralding Him as king.

- ∞ How did Jesus respond to the praise? Did He accept or reject it?

- ∞ Remembering John's purpose, what do you learn from the signs in these chapters?

- ∞ Discuss the contrast between the Light and darkness.

- ∞ What does "now the ruler of this world will be cast out" (John 12:31) mean?

- ∽ Discuss Jesus' washing of the disciples' feet. What does this example teach us about how we should live?

- ∽ Discuss Judas' betrayal. Read John 2:24-25; 6:64. Can we hide things in our hearts from God? What does this mean to you personally?

THOUGHT FOR THE WEEK

Many people think God could never accept them because of what they've done. They think they're beyond anyone's love, and especially God's. This simply means they don't understand God. People like this are basing their opinions on feelings, emotions, or something someone has told them. They certainly aren't shaping them according to the Word and character of God. Others say, "I would love to be loved, but I don't think God really loves me because I've asked Him to do things for me and He hasn't done them." They too misunderstand God and don't know His Word. They don't understand God's extravagant love, which forgives all things and gives everything to us according to our needs.

John will show us Jesus' extravagant love, starting with John 11:54—a turning point from His public ministry among the Jews to a wilderness ministry with His disciples. Passover is at hand, and the Jews are planning to put Him to death.

John 12 reveals Mary's deep love for Jesus. Luke 10:39 tells us that Mary chose to sit at His feet. You won't love God deeply until you sit at the feet of Jesus Christ today by humbly submitting yourself to His Word. Here in John 12, Mary pours ointment worth a year's wages on Jesus' feet. This is a sacrificial investment.

I believe Mary's extravagant love came in response to Jesus' own love and compassion. Remember that when Lazarus died, Jesus wept at the pain of Martha and others. He is touched by our infirmities. His love generates love: "In this is love, not that we loved God, but that He loved us and sent His Son to be the propitiation for our sins" (1 John 4:10). "We love, because He first loved us" (4:19).

So Jesus loves the people around Him, Mary responds accordingly, and what does Judas do? He walks away from the love he has seen revealed so clearly. He kisses Jesus later, but it's a kiss of betrayal. Beloved, never doubt the love of God! When you're tempted to believe He doesn't love you, remember, you *are* beloved.

Jesus' hour, the hour for crucifixion, has come. This is the hour that shows us how much He loves us. Think of it in terms of John 3:16: "For God so loved the world, that He gave His only begotten Son, that whoever believes in Him shall not perish, but have eternal life." If you want to know how much God loves you, look at the cross. God chose to sacrifice His Son for you, and Jesus chose to be sacrificed for you. This is why His hour came. And He was prepared for it. He chose not to pray, "Father, save Me from this hour!"

In chapter 12, John introduces Jesus' hour with Mary anointing Him for burial. Then he reintroduces it with Jesus' ride into Jerusalem on a donkey, when He fulfills the prophecy in Zechariah 9:9: "Behold, your king is coming to you...mounted on a donkey." In those days, when a ruler rode into a city on a donkey, he signified his coming in peace. If he rode toward a city on a white horse, he signified war, and he would normally ride a white horse into a city he conquered. Jesus' first ride signified peace—His coming to lay down His life so that His enemies, you and I, would be reconciled to His Father. "We have peace with God through our Lord Jesus Christ" (Romans 5:1).

His next ride will be on a white horse...to conquer His enemies (Revelation 19:11). If you refuse the Prince of Peace, you will receive the Judge. Jesus' own words will judge you (John 12:48). To choose the Judge is to reject that the Father sent Jesus, that Jesus did His Father's works, and that He spoke His Father's words. Know this: Jesus is coming on a white horse, and He will judge.

Some think, "If He loves me, He won't judge me!" Listen: His provision for you to come to know Him in this life *is* His love. He expressed this love—it's there in history to look at. Jesus laid down His life for His friends and said there is no greater love than this. He laid down His life for us when we were His enemies. If you reject this love, there is no other; all that's left for you is God's just judgment.

The only way we can have life is to have somebody pay the penalty for our sins, which is death. When Jesus Christ hung on the cross, God took away the sin of the world (John 1:29). Jesus breaks the power of the ruler of this world, the devil. Satan has power over you because of your sin. Your sin fuels that power. So if your sin is taken care of, the enemy loses power over you. His power is broken over the course of our day-by-day renewal (2 Corinthians 4:16) and finally when Jesus returns (Philippians 1:6).

Jesus was a man—which is why He's called the Son of Man. He shared in flesh and blood to destroy the devil's power over death with death and to deliver people enslaved to the fear of death. He died so that "through death He might render powerless him who had the power of death, that is, the devil, and might deliver those who through fear of death were subject to slavery all their lives" (Hebrews 2:14-15). Judgment has come, and the prince of this world has been cast out. When we were "dead in [our] trespasses and sins, in which [we] formerly walked according to the course of this world, according to the prince of the power of the air, of the spirit that is now working in the sons of disobedience," we were under the power of the devil (Ephesians 2:1-2). We were by nature children of wrath, under Satan's power. We were under Satan's dominion. He was our father, but when Jesus Christ died, the prince of this world was judged and cast out of this world (John 12:31).

So when you believe in Jesus Christ, you are no longer in Satan's kingdom. You are now in God's kingdom. This is because your sins have been forgiven. The love of God takes you out of the enemy's kingdom, brings you into God's kingdom, makes you alive together with Christ, and raises you up to sit with Him in heavenly places. Speaking of His death, Jesus said, "If I am lifted up from the earth, [I] will draw all men to Myself" (verse 32).

God's extravagant love is light to you. Whenever you walk away from the Word, which tells about His love, you walk away from light and return to darkness. Whenever you walk away from Jesus Christ, you're walking away from the Light. Satan wants you to believe lies. He wants to deceive you. He does not want you to believe that Jesus is the Messiah (Christ), the Son of God. He doesn't want you to have physical life, let alone eternal life. Always remember that Satan is a liar and a murderer; he is malevolent and vicious. He does not live in truth; he wants to keep you away from the Word of God. He wants to keep you blind to the love of God.

In John 13, Jesus faces the cross—His appointed and chosen end: "Having loved His own who were in the world, He loved them to the end." He's about to be made sin for them. He's going to be forsaken by His Father. He's going to drink the full cup of our iniquity. He knows what's coming, and it's troubling Him. But He doesn't focus on the coming crucifixion of His flesh; He focuses rather on the people His Father has chosen and given Him, the ones He loves and cares for, the ones He'll never lose. He'll love them to the end, even the one who is a "devil" (John 6:70), the one who will betray Him with a kiss. Extravagant love!

At the last supper, Jesus arises, covers Himself with a towel, pours water into a basin, and begins to wash and wipe the disciples' feet. Washing the feet of guests before they entered a room was a servant's job, but no servant was present. The disciples had reclined at this table to eat, and suddenly Jesus gets up and becomes the servant. This is too much for Peter, who says, "Never shall You wash my feet!" Jesus answers, "If I don't wash you, you have no part with Me." Then Peter says, "Not only my feet, but also my hands and my head." Jesus responds, "He who has bathed needs only to wash his feet, but is completely clean; and you are clean, but not all of you." One of them had not believed the Word Jesus spoke. Jesus knew who was planning to betray Him, but He washed even *his* feet. Extravagant love!

That's the kind of love God has for you—a love that keeps on giving, that extends as long as you have life and breath, even if you're betraying its Owner. God loves you— it's His very nature; He *is* love. But if you don't accept His love, you will one day experience His wrath.

O Beloved, as long as you live, never doubt God's love for you, even if you've denied or betrayed Him. Don't think that God loves us the way we love—conditionally. We don't naturally love those who reject or betray us.

Precious one, God's revealed love is the only way you can get to God. Jesus said if you don't honor Him, you don't honor His Father. If you reject Him, the Father will reject you. Jew or Gentile, my friend, there's no other way to God than by accepting His eternal love and forgiveness. So become clean—let Him wash you in the blood of the Lamb, the Lamb of God who takes away the sins of the world.

O precious one, don't slap this love in the face. Turn around, love the Father, confess His Son, and speak His gospel to those who dwell in darkness regardless of your personal cost. Don't prefer man's approval to God's. No human will love you unconditionally; only God will. Precious one, you need to confess Jesus Christ, and if you don't, you will face the judgment of God. Have you responded to this love? If you haven't, receive now the gift God sent—His Son. John said, "As many as received Him, to them He gave the right to become the children of God, even to those who believe in His name" (John 1:12). This is the light for your path. Will you believe? Will you receive His love or walk away? The choice is yours.

WHAT ARE YOU PRODUCING?

Does life seem barren, my friend? What are you producing? Is it beneficial? Whom does it benefit? Do the benefits last? How long? You may feel as if you're producing nothing worthwhile. Well, Beloved, it doesn't have to stay that way. You may feel insignificant, but God takes base things, foolish things, despised things, things relatively nothing and uses them mightily…"so that no man may boast before God" (1 Corinthians 1:29).

DAY ONE

Read John 14, watching for time indicators and locations and marking the following key words in distinctive colors or ways: *love, believe,* and *Jesus Christ.* Be sure to mark pronouns that refer to Jesus. (Make sure they refer to Him.)

If someone asks you what John 14 is about, what will you say at this point?

Jesus is in the upper room. When is this happening? If you need to refresh your memory, go back to John 13. Whom is Jesus speaking to? Where's Judas?

DAY TWO

Read John 14 again today. This time mark references to the *Spirit* and corresponding pronouns and synonyms. (Watch carefully for these.)

Remember John's purpose—to reveal certain signs Jesus did so people will believe He is the Christ, the Son of God, and receive life in His name.

From this point on, Jesus does not minister to the public. Instead, He spends time with His disciples. As He approaches His hour (His end), He wants *them particularly* to understand the life He came to give them. He teaches them what to expect, how to live, and who will help them. These are very important chapters. If you understand them, you'll know how to live the abundant life Jesus promised in John 10:10 when you go through the trials He says come on all who are entering God's kingdom (John 16:33).

John 16:33 tells us why Jesus spoke "these things" (in John 13–16) to His disciples. Write the reason in your notebook and keep it in mind as you study these chapters.

Make a list of everything you learn about Jesus Christ in John 14. Record your insights on the chart at the end of week 11 titled WHAT JOHN 14–16 TEACHES ABOUT THE FATHER, SON, AND HOLY SPIRIT, or list them in your notebook now and transfer them later. This will be a long list but an important one.

DAY THREE

List everything you learned about the Holy Spirit in John 14. When you finish, transfer this list to the chart

WHAT JOHN 14-16 TEACHES ABOUT THE FATHER, SON, AND HOLY SPIRIT at the end of week 11.

Now read John 14 and mark every reference to the *Father* and pronouns and synonyms that refer to Him. When you finish, list what you learned about Him from John 14 and record these truths on WHAT JOHN 14-16 TEACHES ABOUT THE FATHER, SON, AND HOLY SPIRIT.

Record a theme for John 14 on JOHN AT A GLANCE in the appendix.

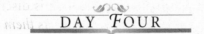

DAY FOUR

Read John 15 today, marking time indicators, locations, and references to the *Father*, the *Son*, and the *Spirit* of truth (the Helper) just as you marked them in John 14.

Now read John 15 again, this time marking key words *abide*,[16] *love*, *hate*, and *world*.

DAY FIVE

List what you learn from John 15 about each person of the Trinity on the chart WHAT JOHN 14-16 TEACHES ABOUT THE FATHER, SON, AND HOLY SPIRIT.

DAY SIX

Biblical authors frequently used figures of speech: a word, phrase, or an expression used in an imaginative way rather than a literal way. Understanding what these are and how they get points across is important for you. John tells the reader in John 10:6 that Jesus used figures of speech. Jesus tells His disciples in John 16:25 that He used figures of speech, and His disciples recognized in John 16:29 when He was not using figurative language.

These are four common figures of speech: metaphor, simile, allegory, and parable.

- A metaphor is an implied comparison. The Gospel of John includes many of these. When Jesus says He is the Light of the world or the bread of life, He's using metaphors to explain what He's like.

- A simile is an explicit comparison, using *like, as, such as,* and other phrases.

- An allegory is a description of one thing using the image of another. Jesus' image of the vine and the branches in John 15, for example, describes different relationships to Jesus Christ.

- A parable is a story that teaches a moral lesson.

John 15:1-9 is an allegory. List in your notebook what you learn about *the vine, the vinedresser,* and *the branches.*

What is this allegory's lesson? To answer this, first answer the following questions:

- To whom is Jesus speaking?

- Who is with Jesus, and what is about to happen to Him?

- Who left the upper room to betray Him (see John 13:21-30)?

- What do you learn about Judas from John 6:66-71 and 13:18?

∞ Did Judas abide in the vine? Did he bear fruit?

∞ Did Judas ever look like he believed in Jesus Christ? When did it become obvious that he really wasn't a true follower?

Do you think Jesus told this allegory to make the disciples understand that not everyone who follows Him truly believes?

Record a theme for John 15 on JOHN AT A GLANCE.

We have more to learn from John 15, but we'll do this next week when we study John 16. Remember, John 13–16 go together. Jesus is preparing His disciples for His death, the coming of the Holy Spirit, and the trouble they will face in the world because they belong to Him.

DAY SEVEN

 Store in your heart: John 14:6

Read and discuss: John 14:15-31; 15:1-17

QUESTIONS FOR DISCUSSION OR INDIVIDUAL STUDY

∞ Discuss what you learned about the Father, Son, and Holy Spirit.

∞ Share what these truths mean to you personally.

∞ Review what you learned from the allegory of the vine and branches.

∞ Discuss what abiding in Jesus means and apply this to the 11 disciples and Judas.

∾ Compare John 15:6 and 15:7. Discuss the importance of God's Word abiding in us.

∾ What do you learn about love from these chapters?
How will you apply this in your life?

THOUGHT FOR THE WEEK

Regardless of who you are, what your education is,
where you came from, or what you have or don't have, all
that matters is whether you are abiding in the vine, which
is Jesus Christ. Do you have a relationship with Him? God
wants you to know how to bear fruit and live a life with
eternal significance, a worthwhile life. This happens only
through a relationship with His Son, described as being "in
the vine."

Christianity is not a religion, it's a relationship. Jesus
illustrates this relationship in chapter 15 with a vine and
branches. People could easily understand this image because
vineyards filled the land of Israel. The vine and branches
illustrate relationships they can have with the Father, with
the Son, and with each other—all to bear fruit. The allegory
also illustrates what happens when a branch is cut out of the
vine. Jesus had 12 followers, but now only 11 are left—one
walked away to betray Him. Jesus had washed Judas's feet,
but Judas left to receive 30 pieces of silver in exchange for
the betrayal.

The context of this allegory shows us its interpretation.
One branch has departed—it did not abide in the vine. It
will not bear fruit; it will wither away to be gathered with
other dead branches and burned.

Judas experienced everything the 11 disciples experienced. He professed faith in Jesus and stayed with Him
even after His "difficult statement" about eating His flesh

(John 6:60) after which "many of His disciples withdrew" (6:66). But now Judas is gone, a branch taken away.

God prunes branches that bear fruit so they will bear more fruit. Accordingly, Jesus told the 11, "You are already clean because of the word which I have spoken to you" (15:3). When Peter told him "Never shall You wash my feet," Jesus said, "If I do not wash you, you have no part with Me" (13:8). From this it seems clear that Judas was never cleansed by Jesus because he never believed in Jesus. He never received the Word. He heard it and could spout it out, but he never received the Word, embracing Him in faith.

Peter immediately repented at the Lord's rebuke: "Lord, then wash not only my feet, but also my hands and my head." Then Jesus said, "He who has bathed needs only to wash his feet." If you're in the vine bearing fruit, God will prune you to produce more, to pare you back, so to speak. *Any* fruit that you bear signifies that you're abiding in Him, that you're connected to Him. No fruit at all means you have no relationship with Jesus and His Father.

Now look at Jesus' words in John 13:10-11. "'You are clean, but not all of you.' For He knew the one who was betraying Him; for this reason He said, 'Not all of you are clean.'" Verse 18 is equally strong: "I do not speak of all of you. I know the ones I have chosen; but it is that the Scripture may be fulfilled, 'He who eats My bread has lifted up his heel against Me.'"

Christianity is not following Jesus for a while and then turning away to do your own thing. True Christianity is permanent—abiding in the vine and bearing fruit. Fruit proves you're attached to the vine. So catch this: You *will* bear fruit. No fruit; no abiding. No abiding; no genuine faith. Jesus adds, "For apart from me you can do nothing" (15:5).

In John 14:10 Jesus says, "Do you not believe that I am in the Father, and the Father is in Me? The words that I say to you I do not speak on My own initiative, but the Father abiding in Me does His works." It's the same way for Him: Jesus abode in the Father, and the Father produced fruit. You abide in the vine, and He produces fruit in you: "If anyone loves Me, he will keep My word; and My Father will love him, and We will come to him and make Our abode with him" (14:23). True Christianity means you are in the Father and the Father is in you producing fruit to His glory. O precious one, if your life is barren, examine your relationship with the Lord Jesus Christ. Maybe He's not in you and you're not in Him, but it doesn't have to stay that way. He wants your life to be productive, and He wants you to believe on Him.

Abiding and obedience go hand in hand. The fruit of abiding is obedience. In John 14:15 Jesus says, "If you love Me, you will keep My commandments." If I truly love God, I will obey Him. No obedience; no love. No love; no abiding. Obedience defines true love.

Jesus repeats this in John 14:21: "He who has My commandments and keeps them is the one who loves Me; and he who loves Me will be loved by My Father, and I will love him and will disclose Myself to him."

"Just as the Father has loved Me, I have also loved you; abide in My love" (John 15:9). *Abide* means to dwell in, to be at home in. When you come to know Jesus Christ, when you believe on Him, God comes and makes His home in you. He puts His Holy Spirit in you.

"A new commandment I give to you, that you love one another, even as I have loved you, that you also love one another. By this will all men know that you are My disciples, if you have love for one another" (John 13:34-35).

Here's what John is saying: God is love. Jesus is God. Jesus is the vine. I'm the branch. If God is love, which means Jesus is love, then what's going to flow through me? Love! I have the Holy Spirit in me. The Holy Spirit connected me to the vine, putting me into the body of Jesus Christ. Now what's the fruit of the Spirit? Love, joy, peace, and the like! So love is going to flow through me.

Why does Jesus say, "A new commandment I give to you"? What's new about love? In the Old Testament, God commanded His people to love Him with their whole heart, soul, mind, and strength. Jesus Himself said this is the first and greatest commandment, and He said loving our neighbors as ourselves is the second. So what's new? It's this: We're not to love our neighbors as we love ourselves. We're to love our neighbors the way He loved us. He's taking us to a much higher level. It's love far beyond ourselves. It's loving with the love Jesus Christ demonstrated when He gave His life: "Greater love has no one than this, that one lay down his life for his friends" (John 15:13). The love He's calling us to now is to lay down our lives for our brethren, His sheep. "You are My friends, if you do what I command you" (verse 14).

Have you ever heard someone say something like this? "Listen, I'm a Christian. Leave me alone. I know I'm going to heaven. I walked an aisle. I prayed a prayer." You say, "But what about obedience?" And he says, "Look, as long as I believe, I'm a Christian." But you look at his life and don't see any fruit.

If your life is barren, you're not connected to the vine—that's what Jesus says. True Christians are in relationship with Jesus Christ. The life of Jesus Christ flows through them, and they produce fruit. That is, they obey. Obedience produces a lifestyle different from the world's, one the world hates. The world is going to hate and persecute you when you know Christ and abide in Him.

If He chose you and appointed you to bear fruit, you *will* bear fruit. If you never bear fruit, He never chose or appointed you. It's as simple as that.

O precious one, do you have a relationship with Christ? If you do, the world will hate you, but oh, the Father is ever going to love you. I want to leave you with this special word. In John 15:24-25, Jesus says, "If I had not done among them the works which no one else did, they would not have sin; but now they have both seen and hated Me and My Father as well. But they have done this to fulfill the word that is written in their Law, 'They hated Me without a cause.'" If the world hates you, you need to make sure it's *without a cause*. That means the world hates you not because you're like it (evil) but rather because you're different from it. That difference is the love of God flowing through you, even to your enemies. The world does not love its enemies. Cut off from the vine, our world is filled with conflict and war everywhere. O precious one, abide in the vine and produce that fruit the world can't stand...and yet needs in order to be saved.

CAN I HAVE AN INTIMATE RELATIONSHIP WITH GOD?

O my friend, let me ask you a question. Do you think you can possibly have an intimate relationship with God? A relationship where you talk to Him, commune with Him, feel Him leading you? John gives the answer.

DAY ONE

Read John 14–15 again today. You're about to see Jesus speak to the 11 disciples after He washed their feet and ate with them. Mark every reference to the 11 disciples. Watch for and mark pronouns that refer to them.

DAY TWO

Make a list of everything you learned from marking the references to the 11. Transfer this to the chart WHAT JOHN 14–16 TEACHES ABOUT THOSE WHO COME TO THE FATHER THROUGH THE SON. This chart is found at the end of week 11.

Should what you listed about the 11 disciples be true of you, if you belong to the Lord Jesus Christ? Why?

DAY THREE

Read John 16. Look for time indicators and locations, and mark every reference to *God* (the Father), *Jesus Christ,* and the *Holy Spirit,* including synonyms and pronouns. You don't want to miss a single precious truth. Also mark the key words *believe* and *love.*

DAY FOUR

Now list everything you learned from marking the references to Jesus Christ on the chart WHAT JOHN 14–16 TEACHES ABOUT THE FATHER, SON, AND HOLY SPIRIT.

List everything you learned about the Father and the Holy Spirit and record these on the chart WHAT JOHN 14–16 TEACHES ABOUT THE FATHER, SON, AND HOLY SPIRIT. Watch for three things the Holy Spirit does when He comes.

DAY FIVE

Examine the following passages with the 5 W's and H to see what they teach about the Holy Spirit. Note where the Spirit goes, what He does, and why. You may want to mark these three things in the text of your Bible by putting a number above each one. This is a good way to mark lists right in your Bible. It helps you observe the text closely and remember what God says. Add insights to the chart WHAT JOHN 14–16 TEACHES ABOUT THE FATHER, SON, AND HOLY SPIRIT.

> John 1:32-33
>
> John 3:5-6,8
>
> John 3:34
>
> John 4:23-24
>
> John 6:63
>
> John 7:38-39
>
> John 20:22

According to what you just learned, if you believe on the Lord Jesus Christ, where is the Holy Spirit with respect to you? Review all you learned about the Holy Spirit from your chart WHAT JOHN 14–16 TEACHES ABOUT THE FATHER, SON, AND HOLY SPIRIT. Then thank God for all He will do for you through the Holy Spirit. Tell Him you want to remember this and live in light of these truths.

DAY SIX

Read through John 16 again, this time marking references to the 11 disciples Jesus chose.

List what you learned on the chart WHAT JOHN 14–16 TEACHES ABOUT THOSE WHO COME TO THE FATHER THROUGH THE SON.

Record a theme for John 16 on JOHN AT A GLANCE.

DAY SEVEN

Store in your heart: John 16:33
Read and discuss: John 16

QUESTIONS FOR DISCUSSION OR INDIVIDUAL STUDY

- Discuss your insights about the Father, Son, and Holy Spirit from John 16.

- Review what you learned about the Holy Spirit from John 1–14.

- Discuss what you learned from John 14–16 about those who come to the Father through Jesus Christ.

- What's the cost of following Jesus? How does the world respond to those who follow Him?

- Discuss how Jesus prepared His disciples for tribulation. What tribulation have you faced or are you facing? What can you expect to face in the future in light of John 15:19?

- Why is loving one another important?

- How do these things apply to your daily life?

THOUGHT FOR THE WEEK

You can have an intimate relationship with God through the person of the Holy Spirit. Remember Nicodemus in John 3? We learned from his story that we need to be born again—born of the Spirit: "Truly, truly, I say to you, unless one is born of water and the Spirit, he cannot enter into the kingdom of God. That which is born of flesh is flesh" (John

3:5). Flesh and blood, Paul tells us in 1 Corinthians 15:50, will not inherit the kingdom of God, so we must have the Spirit within us. According to 1 Corinthians 12:13, "For by [in] one Spirit we were all baptized into one body, whether Jews or Greeks, whether slaves or free, we were all made to drink of one Spirit." There's only one Spirit, the Holy Spirit, and when you believe in Jesus Christ you are baptized in the Spirit into His body. To be baptized primarily means to identify with. When cloths were dyed in Jesus' days, they took the character of the dye they were immersed in. This is what Jesus means by the new birth—we are born of the Spirit and put into His body. We identify with Him: "The one who joins Himself to the Lord is one spirit with Him" (1 Corinthians 6:17).

Now when you and I are saved and baptized into the body of Christ, we receive the Holy Spirit. Jesus told the woman in Samaria, "An hour is coming, and now is, when the true worshipers will worship the Father in spirit and truth; for such people the Father seeks to be His worshipers. God is Spirit, and those who worship Him must worship Him in spirit and truth" (John 4:23-24). So God is Spirit—we worship Him in truth and in the Spirit we're baptized in.

Jesus said, "It is the Spirit who gives life; the flesh profits nothing" (John 6:63). That's why men must be born again. What is born of the flesh is flesh, but what is born of the Spirit is Spirit. "The words that I have spoken to you are spirit and are life" (6:63). The words Jesus Christ speaks are not ordinary words. They are life-giving words. Life comes only through the Spirit—His Spirit, His words. The Spirit gives life to those who are dead in trespasses and sins.

John 7:39 says, "But this He spoke of the Spirit, whom those who believed in Him were to receive; for the Spirit was not yet given, because Jesus was not yet glorified." You and I have an opportunity to have a relationship with God the Father that people in the Old Testament couldn't have.

We ordinary men and women can have an intimate relationship with God by the Spirit.

Now, how do we get the Holy Spirit? When Jesus told His disciples He was about to leave, they were troubled even though He had told them about the Comforter, the Holy Spirit, whom He would send to them. They heard but didn't understand. In the Old Testament, the Spirit came upon kings, priests, and prophets occasionally but never permanently. He came and departed. So the words didn't sink in: "I will ask the Father, and He will give you another Helper, that He may be with you forever" (John 14:16). The Spirit comes alongside to help.

In John 7, John comments, "The Spirit was not yet given, because Jesus was not yet glorified." What does He mean? Well, the Holy Spirit could not indwell people until Jesus made atonement for sin through His death on the cross, rose, and ascended into heaven. Once there and receiving the Spirit Himself, He poured it out on believers (Acts 2:33). The Spirit could now indwell people of faith for the first time in history, and not just leaders but everyone—male and female, bond and free, young and old. The New Covenant of grace replaced the Old Covenant of Law. The Old Covenant was a schoolmaster, a tutor to lead to Christ. It kept people in line until Messiah, Jesus Christ, came. Believers put their faith in the promise of Messiah. The Law showed them their sin (as it shows us today) but did nothing about it.

Jeremiah prophesied that God would make a new covenant with the houses of Israel and Judah unlike the covenant He made with their fathers when He took them out of Egypt, a covenant they broke even though He was their husband, they His bride (Jeremiah 31:31-34). This former covenant was the Mosaic Law. The new covenant would put God's law in the hearts of believers. He would become their God and they His people. They would all know Him. The least to the greatest would all have an intimate relationship with Him because He would forgive their iniquity and no longer remember their sin.

Acts quotes Joel's prophecy that God would pour out His Spirit on all mankind. This happened at the feast of Pentecost. God poured out His Spirit to do something. Ezekiel 36:26-27 promises a new heart, a new spirit, and God's own Spirit to cause each of us to walk in His statutes and observe His commandments. When Jesus Christ says keeping His commandments is abiding in His love, we have to understand that the "keeping" or "abiding" is the fruit of the Holy Spirit within, who starts His work by giving us new hearts and spirits. The Holy Spirit is our power pack inside, our energizer.

So whatever the difficulty, God is present in the power of the Holy Spirit. The Holy Spirit is your sustainer, comforter, helper, and guide to all truth. He reproduces the life of Christ in you and through you. He enables you to love. Apart from Him you can do nothing; with Him you can do all things through Christ who strengthens you.

Regardless of what comes your way, the Holy Spirit is with you, and He will not leave you. Second Corinthians 3:2-3 says we are a letter "written not with ink but with the Spirit of the living God, not on tables of stone [like the old covenant] but on tablets of human hearts." As Ezekiel's prophecy said, "I will take the heart of stone out of their flesh and give them a heart of flesh" (Ezekiel 11:19).

Once you see that you're a sinner, come to the Lord Jesus Christ, and believe on Him, the Holy Spirit comes in and seals you until the day of redemption. You are sealed in Christ "with the Holy Spirit of promise" (Ephesians 1:13). We saw that He was promised in the Old Testament. The Holy Spirit pledges (guarantees) our inheritance, our going to heaven to be with Christ in a brand-new body. Paul says absence from the body is presence with the Lord (2 Corinthians 5:8). But someday the Holy Spirit will generate a new body for your spirit. He's going to take your mortal body and make it immortal. Jesus will fashion your new body to conform with His own. What is corruptible will become incorruptible, that which is mortal will be immortal, and you will be clothed with a brand-new body even as Jesus Christ had a brand-new body. This is His promise to us; this is what the Holy Spirit is all about.

For now, Jesus does not leave you alone. He gives you His Helper, His Comforter. He doesn't leave you without someone who will come to your aid. The Comforter will stay with you forever, He will see that you go straight to heaven when you die, and He will give you a brand-new body when Jesus returns (1 Corinthians 15:52-53). He is the guarantor of your redemption.

Romans 8:15-17 tells us that sons of God "have not received a spirit of slavery leading to fear again, but…a spirit of adoption as sons by which we cry out, 'Abba! Father!' The Spirit Himself testifies with our spirit that we are children of God, and if children, heirs also, heirs of God and fellow heirs with Jesus Christ."

Whatever you suffer will not be worthy to compare with the glory that will be revealed. You can know that you're going to see Jesus' glory if His Spirit is in you. You can't see or know the Spirit apart from Jesus Christ.

Do you know what makes a Christian different from the rest of the world? The indwelling Holy Spirit! When He indwells you, you have so many things the world does not have. You have the abundant life Jesus promised. He seals you until the day of your redemption. He teaches you all things and brings to your memory all Jesus said. The Holy Spirit comes inside to teach you particularly about Him. He's going to teach you more and more about Jesus Christ, more and more about the Father. Why? To help you become more intimate with Him!

LEGACY

What's the greatest legacy you can leave your family and loved ones? Legacies seem to be more important as we get older. That's when we really appreciate our experiences and what we've learned. That's when we start to think back over our lives.

DAY ONE

Read John 17. When you finish, ask the 5 W's and an H and record your insights. Make sure you note who is speaking, what He is speaking about, and to whom.

DAY TWO

Read John 17 again and mark time indicators and locations. Also mark the following key words and pronouns that refer to them: *world, word, eternal life, love,* and *Jesus Christ.*

DAY THREE

Read John 17 again, marking the following key words and phrases:

whom You have given

references to the 11 disciples

Judas

one

glory

love

Do you think Jesus' prayer is just for the 11 disciples or for you as well? (Look for hints in the text.) Now that you have marked the text of John 17, read it again and think about this question. Write down your answer and relevant scriptures.

DAY FOUR

Read John 17 again. Reading the chapter aloud will help you remember it. As a matter of fact, when you read Scripture aloud over and over again, you will find yourself automatically remembering it.

List everything you learn from marking references to Jesus in this chapter. Record your insights on the chart WHAT JOHN 14–16 TEACHES ABOUT THE FATHER, SON, AND HOLY SPIRIT at the end of this lesson.

DAY FIVE

Go through John 17 verse by verse and make a list of everything Jesus says about and prays for the 11 disciples. Then list what He says about and prays for those who believe on Him through their (the disciples') word.

DAY SIX

What is the setting of John 17? Jesus is praying to His Father on your behalf just before He goes to the Garden of Gethsemane. There He'll be arrested and taken to the house of Caiaphas, the high priest, who (with his father-in-law Annas) wants to get rid of Him.

- ∾ From all you have seen in John 13–17, who is uppermost on Jesus' heart?

- ∾ What does this tell you about Him?

- ∾ What does this tell you about what He thinks about you?

Use what you learned from John 17:14-17 to answer these questions:

- ∾ What is the importance of studying the Bible?

- ∾ What do these verses tell you about the Bible?

- ∾ When you finish this study, will you continue studying the Bible? Why?

Record a theme for John 17 on JOHN AT A GLANCE.

DAY SEVEN

 Store in your heart: John 17:15-17
Read and discuss: John 17

QUESTIONS FOR DISCUSSION OR INDIVIDUAL STUDY

- ᴄᴠ Discuss your insights from Jesus' prayer for the 11 disciples and for those who will believe through their word.

- ᴄᴠ How you can model Jesus' prayer?

- ᴄᴠ What did you learn about the importance of God's Word?

- ᴄᴠ How does this compare to what you learned earlier in John?

- ᴄᴠ How is Satan connected to this world? What assurance does this chapter give you with respect to the evil one? What is your responsibility?

THOUGHT FOR THE WEEK

Why did Jesus leave the Upper Room and take the disciples to the Garden of Gethsemane? Why did He talk to the Father on the way? Why did He speak to His Father out loud so the disciples would hear Him?

According to John 17:13, Jesus did this so "they may have My joy made full in themselves"—joy in knowing that they were uppermost in Jesus' heart and joy in knowing what He prayed for them. When you know people are praying for you, for your sanctification or for difficult decisions you have to make, you know you're uppermost in their hearts and minds. Knowing what they're asking God to do can encourage you to think, *I can make it!* Somebody gave me a framed truth that says, "Right now Jesus Christ is at the right hand of the Father interceding for Kay." That's true for you too! We see it for ourselves in Jesus' prayer.

So Jesus prays aloud so His disciples will hear His awesome prayer. We call Matthew 6:9-13 the Lord's Prayer. But actually Jesus is not praying there; He's teaching His disciples how to pray. In John 17, however, Jesus is actually praying for His current disciples and then for all who will believe through their word. Those who never come to Christ are not the subject of this prayer—it's only for those the Father gave the Son.

John 17 is usually referred to as Jesus' high priestly prayer. He had already told His disciples why He said to them the things He said in chapters 13–16: "These things I have spoken to you, so that in Me you may have peace. In the world you have tribulation, but take courage; I have overcome the world" (John 16:33). So you can know this: You're in the world, where God wants you. He isn't going to take you. When He saves you, He saves you from the world but leaves you in it. You're going to have tribulation there—all sorts of pressures of various sizes and shapes that come at you different ways.

A bad legacy may be one of these pressures. But He says you'll have peace in Him. He wants you where He's working, among everything He owns.

Just before Jesus prays for His sheep, He emphasizes the truth that those the Father gave Him have eternal life. He describes eternal life in John 17:3 in terms of knowing the only true God and Jesus Christ whom the Father sent. Then He says, "I glorified You on the earth, having accomplished the work which You have given Me to do." This is what we want to be able to say to the Lord when we see Him face-to-face: "I finished the work You gave me to do." Ephesians 2:10 says, "We are His workmanship, created in Christ Jesus for good works, which God prepared beforehand so that we would walk in them."

Then Jesus asks the Father to glorify Him together with Himself, with the glory He had with the Father before the world was. Before the world came into being, Jesus was with the Father. The first verse in the book told us, "In the beginning was the Word, and the Word was with God, and the Word was God." The Word was in the beginning with the Father in glory. Then He came down. That was another glory—the glory of obedience in becoming the Lamb of God. Wouldn't you love to see the glory He had in the beginning? Wouldn't you love to see the glory of the Father, Son, and Holy Spirit?

Jesus goes on to say in verse 6 that He revealed God's name to the men God gave Him out of the world. Remember, Jesus came to His own, the Jews, and they rejected Him. The world doesn't come to Him because it lies in darkness— it doesn't want its dark deeds exposed to a light that will display what they are. But the Father has given a group of people in the world to the Son. And listen, precious one: If you believe in Jesus Christ, you're part of that group because the Father gave you to the Son. It's awesome to think that out of this mass of mankind, God chose you.

When did you first belong to God? Knowing these truths is part of your legacy. The world doesn't know them. Some Christians don't know them, and others find it hard to understand them. These truths are hard for them to grasp. But if you study the Word of God and mark all the scriptures that tell you God chose you, that He gave you to Jesus Christ, and that He initiates salvation, you will be absolutely awed.

Ephesians 1:4 says God chose us in Christ before the foundation of the world. And He chose us so that "we would be holy and blameless before Him." Isn't this awesome? Before creation, when God first spoke, the Father and Son dwelling in glory chose you. They determined when you would be born and whom you would be born to. And "God predestined us to adoption as sons through Jesus Christ to Himself, according to the kind intention of His will, to the praise of the glory of His grace, which He freely bestowed on us in the Beloved" (Ephesians 1:5-6). The Father gave you to Jesus Christ so that you would receive forgiveness of sins and eternal life and live with Him forever and ever. These are truths for every single child of God.

What about those *not* chosen? Well, what do we know about God? We know God is righteous and just in all His ways, so we can't adversely judge Him or His Word. We simply have to bow the knee, accept, and trust. You may ask, "Does this mean I don't have to witness to anyone?" No, you should witness because that's what He has told you to do. And if His Spirit is dwelling in you, you *will* witness—in fact, you're witnessing one way or the other 24/7. He will both prompt and use your witness to bring people to Jesus Christ.

Now, Jesus said those the Father gave Him "have kept Your word" (John 17:6). If you're truly born again, you will abide in (keep) His Word. That's how we prove we're His disciples. Does this mean we'll never do anything wrong? No, we still sin, but sin is no longer the habit of our life. It's no longer the governing force of our life. We're no longer slaves to sin.

Jesus gave His followers God's words. They understood and received the truth that God sent His Son into the world. John uses *sent* with respect to Jesus about 40 times in his Gospel. Now think back: Why did John write? So readers would believe Jesus is the Christ (Messiah), the Son of God, and receive life in His name. The Father sent Jesus to explain Him. Eternal life is knowing the Father and the Son He sent. If we reject the Son, we reject the Father.

If we don't honor the Son, we don't honor the Father. What is John saying? He's saying the Father and Son are one. Remember that! Precious one, you are part of a very important family. You're part of the family of God because God chose you out of the world. Jesus prayed for you, and John recorded the prayer so you would know what He prayed and see how precious you are to Him…so your joy would be full.

What kind of legacy can you leave your loved ones? You may say, "I'm not rich." Oh, but precious one, you can leave them the legacy of a marked-up Bible and a life devoted to Jesus Christ. And you can write out a prayer for them from your heart. Ask God what to pray and then write it out. Seal it up and leave it for them. Someday after Jesus returns, you'll know how much God used it.

We're called to reveal harmony to a world of chaos—a harmony where people can come to be loved, protected, and nourished. That's what the true church is, my friend, though you may have to look hard to find it. Jesus prayed that we would be one even as the Father and Son are one. This unity, this true church that is one and against which the gates of hell will not prevail, lies behind the many denominations. The unity is produced by the power of the Holy Spirit, causing obedience to the Word of God, according to Jeremiah's and Ezekiel's descriptions of the New Covenant.

What can we learn from Jesus' prayer in John 17? Jesus successfully completed God's work for Him; He manifested God's name, and He gave His sheep God's Word. Then He left to be with the Father. He didn't leave His sheep comfortless; He gave them the Holy Spirit. And because He left them in the world, He prayed that they will be kept in His

Father's name, that God will keep them from the evil one. Satan prances about like a roaring lion to devour people, but Jesus has prayed for you, asking the Father, "Keep them from the evil one." Don't ever forget this, Beloved!

He also prayed that we will be sanctified in God's truth. There's a connection here. How can we be kept from the evil one? One way is by the Word of God. Paul says we're in a war, not against flesh and blood but against principalities, spiritual wickedness in high places, the prince (ruler) of this world. So He tells us to put on the full armor of God (Ephesians 6). He begins with the purpose for the armor: "so that you will be able to resist in the evil day, and having done everything, to stand firm." How do we conquer the evil one? By girding our loins with truth!

Now, returning to John 17, watch what Jesus says: "Sanctify them in the truth; Your word is truth." What does *sanctify* mean? It means to set apart, to differentiate. He's asking the Father to set His followers apart from the world by truth, the truth that the Father sent the Son into the world to save it (John 12:47). We need to speak this truth to the world so that people will believe and receive abundant life, eternal life.

Jesus prayed for our unity. Think about how the Father and Son work together, how the Son always and only did the things that pleased the Father (John 8:29), not Himself (Romans 15:3). He honored the Father, so the Father honored Him. And that's what we're called to do. When we do this, when we are one, the world believes (John 17:21) and knows (17:23) God has sent us.

Jesus also prayed that we would be where He is and see the glory His Father gave Him. What did His first followers see? They watched Jesus go from popularity to condemnation—for being supposedly illegitimate, blaspheming, and demon-possessed. He was despised and rejected, filled with sorrow, and acquainted with grief, as Isaiah prophesied. His followers watched religious leaders tear Him down and plan to get rid of Him. This is what they saw. They saw Him reviled and physically abused.

But Jesus' final prayer guaranteed that they would end up with Him and behold His glory. And that promise extends to all who believe through their word—that's us! Someday, like those in heaven (Revelation 5) who see the Lamb who is worthy to open the sealed scroll, we're going to say, "Worthy is the Lamb!" And we're going to be with Him and see His glory forever. This was His prayer, and it will come to pass.

WHAT JOHN 14–16 TEACHES ABOUT THE FATHER, SON, AND HOLY SPIRIT

The Father	The Son	The Holy Spirit

WHAT JOHN 14–16 TEACHES ABOUT THOSE WHO COME TO THE FATHER THROUGH THE SON

BECAUSE HE LOVES YOU

Has anyone ever told you, my friend, that Jesus Christ died for you? Do you believe He died for you, and do you know all that entails? Can you comprehend the humiliation from men—cursing, spitting, scourging, and the torment of being cursed (Galatians 3:13) and forsaken (Matthew 27:46) in the abyss (Romans 10:7) *because of* you and yet *for* you? He did it because He loves you.

DAY ONE

Read John 18 today and record in the margins of your Bible what happens in each paragraph and where it happens. Remember how we see the start of a paragraph. In the NASB, you'll see the letter A in bold type in the middle of verse 38. This means a new paragraph starts there. Also remember that a paragraph is a group of sentences with a common thought or event.

Now read through John 18 again, this time marking references to time and location. All the events happen in Jerusalem, but mark the different places in the city. In the appendix, consult the map that shows Jerusalem at the time of Jesus to see where these places are.

Read John 18:33-40 again, marking the key words *truth, king,* and *kingdom.* Mark *king* the way you did in John 12, but mark *kingdom* differently.

DAY TWO

Read John 19 today and follow the directions from yesterday about paragraph content and references to time and location. Mark *truth*[17] and *king* again and add *sin.*

DAY THREE

Read John 18 again paragraph by paragraph, but this time focus on individuals who interact with Jesus. Watch what each person does and how Jesus responds to him. If the text explains *why* Jesus responded the way He did, note these explanations. Record in your notebook your insights about interactions between these people:

- Jesus and Judas
- Jesus and Peter
- Jesus and the high priest and his officers
- Jesus and Pilate

DAY FOUR

Read John 19 today paragraph by paragraph, focusing on individuals who interact with Jesus. Again, list insights regarding interactions between these people:

- Jesus and Pilate (add this to your list from John 18)

- Jesus and the Jews

- Jesus and the chief priests

- Jesus and the soldiers

- Jesus and His mother

- Jesus and Joseph of Arimathea

- Jesus and Nicodemus (remember Nicodemus from John 3? What does this imply about Nicodemus?)

DAY FIVE

Look at the key words you marked this week—*sin, truth,*[18] *king,* and *kingdom.* List in your notebook what you learned about each from John 18–19.

Record themes for John 18 and 19 on JOHN AT A GLANCE.

DAY SIX

Read John 18–19 again. Think about all that happened and picture the events in your mind. As you do, remember that Jesus is God. God planned the events (Luke 22:22; Acts 2:23; 4:27-28). Jesus had the power to stop the Roman guards from beating and crucifying Him, but He didn't. Why? These events are part of the sacrificial atonement God ordained from eternity. Review what you learned about the grain of wheat falling to the ground, the fruit of the vine, the Good Shepherd laying down His life, the Lamb of God, the Passover Lamb, the Light of the world, the One who calls those who are thirsty to drink of Him, and the King who rides into Jerusalem on a donkey.

Then spend some time worshipping God for what He planned and did for you, Beloved. Kneel before Him, pray a prayer of thanksgiving, and praise Him.

DAY SEVEN

 Store in your heart: John 19:36-37
Read and discuss: John 18–19

QUESTIONS FOR DISCUSSION OR INDIVIDUAL STUDY

- ∾ Discuss John 18–19 paragraph by paragraph, focusing on the order of events.

- ∾ Discuss how each character or group interacted with Jesus, and note His responses. What do you learn about Jesus, people, and how to respond to others?

- ∾ Discuss what you learned about *sin, truth,* the *king,* and the *kingdom.*

- ∾ What struck you most deeply about Jesus in these events? How can you use this knowledge to be more like Him?

THOUGHT FOR THE WEEK

Maybe you've heard Jesus loves you and you've wondered, *How? How does He love me?* Maybe you've heard, "He died for you," but all you could think was, *Oh, He died.*

You've been blindsided. Try to focus on the truth that He died *for you.* Jesus Christ is the King, and the King died...for you. This may be difficult for you to accept because kings reign; they don't give up their lives. Well, this king was very different.

When Jesus enters the Praetorium (John 18:28), Pilate summons Him.

> "Are You the King of the Jews?"
>
> Jesus answered, "Are you saying this on your own initiative, or did others tell you about Me?"
>
> Pilate answered, "I am not a Jew, am I? Your own nation and the chief priests delivered You to me; what have You done?"
>
> Jesus answered, "My kingdom is not of this world. If My kingdom were of this world, then My servants would be fighting so that I would not be handed over to the Jews; but as it is, My kingdom is not of this realm."

These last words explain why Jesus told Peter to put up his sword. He was demonstrating that the battle would not be won that way. It would be won by Jesus laying down His life because that's how He would defeat the prince of this world, the prince of darkness. When He was lifted up, the prince of this world was cast down.

Pilate didn't understand the nature of the truth or of the kingdom Jesus was talking about. To him, truth was relative. But my friend, there are absolutes. Black and white *do* exist—what God says is truth is absolute truth. Anything you read in His book is pure truth. Now, when Pilate asked if he should release the King of the Jews, this irritated the Jews, who demanded he exchange Jesus for another prisoner: "So they cried out again, saying, 'Not this Man, but Barabbas.'" They preferred this thief to Jesus, the King of kings. That's what they demanded. The crowd had been set up. Remember, John introduced Jesus as the king of Jews as early as the first chapter: Nathaniel confessed, "Rabbi, You are the Son of God; You are the King of Israel" (John 1:49).

He *is* the king of Israel, and we should never forget this. He's going to reign as Israel's king, and this explains why Israel has endured generations of enemies and will never be wiped out. The covenants, gifts, and calling of God are irrevocable. "The Deliverer will come from Zion, He will remove ungodliness from Jacob" (Romans 11:26). He will deliver His people Israel and set up His kingdom.

When Pilate learned that Jesus was a Galilean, He sent Him to his enemy Herod (Luke 23:7). Even Herod knew of people who claimed Jesus had performed significant miracles. But Jesus didn't respond to Herod's interrogation. So Herod mocked Jesus, dressed Him in a gorgeous robe, and sent Him back to Pilate. Luke records, "Now Herod and Pilate became friends with one another that very day; for before they had been enemies with each other" (23:12). What drew them together? It was the bond of condemning the King of kings to death.

Pilate had Jesus scourged. According to Matthew 27:26-31, they took Jesus to the Praetorium and gathered the Roman cohort around Him. It was the Passover, when Jewish males were required by the Law to gather and celebrate the feast in Jerusalem, and Pilate probably wanted to make sure to avoid a riot.

To pass time, Roman soldiers sometimes played "the king's game." They dressed up a man to look like a king and then abused him. The winner got to abuse him more. The Romans restricted Jews to inflicting 39 stripes for punishment, but they could scourge a man to just short of death. He could be beaten and even mutilated, but his life was spared for crucifixion—their mode for execution.

Now let's see what Jesus endured because He loved you. The soldiers stripped Him and put a scarlet robe on Him. The abuse continued:

> After twisting together a crown of thorns, they put it on His head, and a reed in His right hand; and they knelt down before Him and mocked Him, saying, "Hail, King of the Jews!" They spat on Him, and took the reed and began to beat Him on the head. After they mocked him, they took the scarlet robe off and put His own garments back on Him, and led Him away to crucify Him (Matthew 27:29-31).

The thorns were like very long and sharp nails. Jesus had already been beaten, either by the Sanhedrin or its slaves. Before this He had sweat great drops of blood in the Garden of Gethsemane as His capillaries burst because of the incredible stress of what He was facing. He spent an entire night in the house of Caiaphas, possibly in a cistern. He faced a cruel trial, He was severely beaten, and now He endures more pain from the crown of thorns.

Scourging was commonly done with a stick with nine leather straps. Each strap had two hooks—one on the very end, the other 13 inches up. They were made from metal or bone. The hooks hit a bare back and caught there as the straps wrapped around to the sides and front (abdomen).

When the scourge was pulled back, the flesh ripped and flew off the back and abdomen, and the exposed arteries spit out blood.

> There is a fountain filled with blood
> Drawn from Emmanuel's veins,
> And sinners plunged beneath that flood
> Lose all their guilty stains.

He loves you. He was despised and scourged...for you. Isaiah prophesied, "His appearance was marred more than any man" (52:14). The Hebrew indicates that when the soldiers were through with Him, He was unrecognizable as a man.

Does Jesus love you? Yes, He does. Did He simply die? No, He suffered and died *for you and me.*

You can know He paid the extreme price, so you also know He understands when *you* go through intense suffering.

> He was despised and forsaken of men, a man of sorrows, and acquainted with grief; and like one from whom men hide their face He was despised, and we did not esteem Him. Surely our griefs He Himself bore, and our sorrows he carried; yet we ourselves esteemed Him stricken, smitten of God, and afflicted. But He was pierced through for our transgressions, He was crushed for our iniquities; the chastening of our well-being fell upon Him, and by His scourging we are healed (Isaiah 53:3-5).

Our iniquities fell on Him. As a result, we are healed. What are we healed of? First Peter 2:24-25 tells us. Let Scripture interpret Scripture here, precious one.

He Himself bore our sins in His body on the cross, so that we might die to sin and live to righteousness; for by His wounds you were healed. For you were continually straying like sheep, but now you have returned to the Shepherd and the Guardian of your souls.

We were healed from our sins. His death paid our penalty—we don't have to pay it.

You are precious to Him. You are beloved to Him. Like a silent lamb before shearers, Jesus didn't open His mouth. Why? Because He came into the world for this purpose. God prepared a Passover lamb—the spotless, blameless, Lamb of God.

Every year the Jews killed, roasted, and ate a Passover lamb to recall how blood from a lamb applied to their doorposts and lintels protected their firstborn from death in Egypt. Jesus said, "I am the living bread that came down from heaven; if anyone eats of this bread, he will live forever. And the bread also which I will give for the life of the world is My flesh" (John 6:51). Yes, you're precious. This is *how* precious.

Pilate found no guilt in Jesus, but he delivered Him to be crucified to appease the angry mob of Jews. According to archaeological evidence, crucifixion involved nailing a person's ankles to an upright pole (or tree) and fixing his arms fixed to a crossbar. Normally, it was done on a road where passersby could see what happened to those who disobeyed Rome.

More significantly, God found no guilt in Jesus. You were redeemed with the incorruptible blood of the Lamb of God, a Lamb without spot or blemish, so your sins could be forgiven.

Every word in this book, the Bible, is true. God loves you; you're precious to Him. If you look to this Son of God who died for you, you'll have life—abundant life, eternal life, not just prolonged existence. The Lamb of God died so that you and your loved ones—your mother and father, your children, and your best friends—might not perish but have everlasting life. Jesus is the Lord, the Son of God, God in the flesh, the only way to the Father. Have you truly believed in Him, in all He is and has done? Have you opened your heart and said, "I want to receive You; I want know You, Lord!"

Living Out Truth

What do you do when you've blown it with God? It's one thing to blow it with a human being, but God? That's another story!

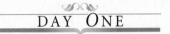

DAY ONE

Read John 19:38 through John 20:31 paragraph by paragraph. Note where the action takes place, when, and who is involved. Mark time indicators and locations.

DAY TWO

Read John 20 again, and mark the following key words: *peace, believe, sins, rise (from the dead), ascend.*[19]

List in your notebook all you learned from marking these key words. Do you see a difference between rising from the dead and ascending? What is it?

DAY THREE

Read John 2:13-22.

∽ How do the main events in this passage and John 20 relate?

∾ What was the final sign God gave to prove that Jesus is the Christ, the Son of God?

∾ Did anyone witness this final sign? Who? When?

Read 1 Corinthians 15:1-8, marking *gospel* and its pronouns with a red megaphone shaded green; . Underline *of first importance*[20] and circle each occurrence of *that*.

DAY FOUR

Read the accounts of the death, burial, and resurrection of our Lord Jesus Christ in the other Gospels: Matthew 27–28; Mark 14–16; and Luke 22–24.

DAY FIVE

Read John 21 paragraph by paragraph, noting what happens, who is involved, and when and where events take place. Make these notes in your notebook.

Read John 21 again. Look for time indicators and locations and mark the following key words: *love, sheep (lambs), testify, testimony, manifested*. Watch for what or who was manifested, how, and when.

List in your notebook what you learn.

DAY SIX

What did you learn from John 21 about Peter?

Reread John 18:15-27. Answer the following questions by comparing these verses with John 21:

∾ What was Peter standing by when he denied Jesus Christ?

∾ What was Peter standing by when Jesus talked with him (John 21:9-19)?

∾ Although Peter denied Jesus three times in John 18, what did he tell Jesus three times in John 21?

∾ What did Peter tell Jesus he would do for Him in John 13:37?

∾ When Jesus was arrested, what did Peter do?

∾ According to John 21, what did Jesus say Peter will face?

∾ Will Peter deny Jesus again? What does the text say or imply?

What does John 21 say about the John who wrote this Gospel?

Finally, record themes for John 20 and 21 on JOHN AT A GLANCE.

Now that you have themes for all chapters on JOHN AT A GLANCE, read them over. Considering John's purpose, which statement describes the book as a whole? This is your theme for the book. Record it on the appropriate place on the chart.

Scan John 1–11 and note the signs Jesus performed. Record these on JOHN AT A GLANCE in the column headed "Signs and Miracles."

Jesus describes Himself metaphorically in many ways in John, such as Light of the world and bread of life. Record these in the appropriate column on JOHN AT A GLANCE.

DAY SEVEN

Store in your heart: John 20:30-31
Read and discuss: John 20–21; 1 Corinthians 15:1-8;
John 3:36; 5:24; 6:39-40

QUESTIONS FOR DISCUSSION OR INDIVIDUAL STUDY

∞ From John 20 and 1 Corinthians 15:1-8, discuss the resurrection. What are the facts and implications?

∞ What proof of the resurrection is given in John 21?

∞ Is the resurrection of Jesus a sign? How does His resurrection compare with Lazarus' in John 11? What are the differences between the two?

∞ What is promised to believers? To unbelievers?

∞ What did you learn about Jesus, Peter, Jesus' sheep, and John?

∞ How did Jesus treat Peter? What was Peter's concern about John, and how did Jesus respond to it? What lesson can you apply to your life?

∞ What did you learn about Christians who die?

∞ What have you learned from this study of John that will impact your life? What truths will affect your relationship with God? What lessons will you commit to live out?

THOUGHT FOR THE WEEK

John 20 details appearances Jesus made following His resurrection. Mary Magdalene was first to see the Lord. She quickly told the disciples about this appearance and what the Lord said to her. The Lord had set her free from "seven demons" (Mark 16:9). She was completely devoted to Him out of appreciation for her release from slavery.

Jesus chose Mary to be the first person to see Him after His resurrection. He gave her the exciting privilege of telling His disciples He rose from the dead!

First Corinthians 15 explains the importance of Jesus' resurrection. Paul says those who are truly saved hold fast to the gospel of the resurrection. In fact, he says, without the resurrection, there is no gospel. If Christ has not been raised, we're still in our sins, those who fall asleep in Christ perish, and faith is worthless (15:17-18).

What is this gospel? The apostle Paul defines it, beginning in 1 Corinthians 15:3: "For I delivered to you as of first importance what I also received, that Christ died for our sins according to the Scriptures." The first three points are these: Christ died, He died for sins, and the Scriptures prophesied these things. The only Scripture God's people had at this time was the Old Testament. The Old Testament prophesied the death of the Messiah.

First Corinthians 15 continues defining the gospel: "He was buried." Burial testifies to the fact that Jesus really died; He didn't "hide out" for a while. Then, "He was raised on the third day according to the Scriptures." So burial and resurrection are part of the gospel, and these too were proclaimed in the Old Testament.

Verse 5 says, "He appeared to Cephas [Peter], then to the twelve. After that He appeared to more than five hundred brethren at one time."

Why is this appearance important? When someone appears to one person here and another there, people can say, "I doubt it. One was on drugs, and the other didn't have his glasses on," or "They want to believe they saw Him." But an appearance to a crowd of 500 people at one time is proof enough. Paul adds that the majority of the 500 were still alive when he wrote, possibly 30 years later (verse 6). Anyone contesting Paul would have to contend with hundreds of eyewitnesses. Paul continues, "Then He appeared to James, then to all the apostles; and last of all, as to one untimely born, He appeared to me also" (verses 7-8).

In Romans 4, Paul says Abraham was justified by faith, that is, declared righteous. Abraham put his faith in the sacrifice of Jesus Christ as he looked forward. (The eternal gospel was preached to Abraham, according to Galatians 3:8.) Now you and I look back to that sacrifice. Romans 4:22-24 says, "It was credited to him as righteousness. Now not for his sake only was it written that it was credited to him, but for our sakes also, to whom it will be credited, as those who believe in Him who raised Jesus our Lord from the dead."

No righteousness is credited to your account before God if you do not believe the gospel—that Jesus Christ died for your sins, that He was buried, and that He was raised from the dead. Paul says, "He [Jesus]...was delivered over because of our transgressions, and was raised because of our justification" (Romans 4:25). So Christ hung on the cross for our transgressions. He was raised because God accepted His offering for sin in our place. Jesus was made sin for us (2 Corinthians 5:21) and offered Himself as a sin offering (Hebrews 9:14). According to Romans 6, God crucified us *with* Christ and *in* Christ. He saw us in the tomb in Christ and raised in Him to walk in newness of life. That resurrection is our release from slavery to sin, our freedom. We are declared righteous in Him. In Him we receive the Holy Spirit, further testimony to the fact that our sins are forgiven and to the power that enables us to live godly lives and share the gospel with others.

Three times Jesus said to His followers, "Peace be with you" (John 20:19,21,26). That's because the enmity that separated them from God was gone and they had peace with God (Romans 5:1). You see, sin separates us from God (Isaiah 59:2). "The mind set on the flesh is hostile toward God" (Romans 8:7). But when Jesus Christ died on the cross, He paid for your sins, so you're no longer an enemy of God. The hostility, hatred, and anger are gone, and you have peace with Him.

So even if you've blown it with God, you can have peace with Him because of Jesus' death, burial, resurrection, and ascension. Consider Peter. He denied Jesus three times after promising he would never deny Him and would in fact die with Him if necessary. He boasted that the others might deny Jesus, but Peter was confident he never would. Still he did. His spirit was willing, but his flesh was weak. In the Garden of Gethsemane he slept, and at Caiaphas' house he denied knowing Jesus. And he wept bitterly afterward. Imagine how he felt when he heard "Peace be to you" three times—offsetting his three denials!

Jesus revealed Himself to Peter on a day Peter was failing at fishing, his profession. He told him what to do to catch fish, to be successful (a repeat of the catch in Luke 5). And He built a fire. Where did Peter stand when he denied Jesus? By a fire. Peter recognizes his sinfulness (as he did in Luke 5:8) and that Jesus can teach him a thing or two about fishing—for fish or men.

Whenever we walk in the flesh, we produce its works, works that cannot please God. So when you're tempted and start to walk away, remember this: you're sowing to the flesh, and that will reap corruption. You can do nothing of eternal significance without Him, so you need to be filled with His Spirit. If you are not filled with the Spirit, you will walk in the flesh and produce the works of the flesh.

Jesus questioned Peter: "'Simon, son of John, do you love Me more than these?' He said to Him, 'Yes, Lord; You know that I love You.' He said to him, 'Tend My lambs.'" Now watch. Three times Jesus asks Peter, "Do you love Me?" How many times did Peter deny Jesus? Three times! For those three denials Jesus gives him three opportunities to prove his love by feeding His sheep. What is Jesus doing? He's keeping the door to repentance open. Jesus is taking Peter back to his denial and allowing him to confess his love for Jesus Christ and to make his commitment to follow Jesus Christ. So go back to that time when you failed God, when you blew it. Then make a new commitment to Him that will prove Your love—commit to feed His sheep.

What can you do, my friend, when you've blown it with God? You begin by realizing that if you're a child of God, God is not finished with you. He's the great Redeemer. He's the great Restorer. He still has work for you to do. If He didn't, you'd be gone.

> "Truly, truly I say to you, when you were younger, you used to gird yourself and walk wherever you wished; but when you grow old, you will stretch out your hands and someone else will gird you, and bring you where you do not wish to go." Now this He said, signifying by what kind of death he would glorify God (John 21:18-19).

Peter had said earlier he would die with Jesus if necessary, and now Jesus prophesies that it *will* happen. Then He told Peter, "Follow Me!"

This is God's closing word to you, precious one, wherever you are, whoever you are. If you're lost, He's saying to you, "Deny yourself, take up your cross, and follow Me. Believe that I am the Christ, the Son of God. Become My child, become My disciple, become My follower, My student. If you've blown it, go back. Repent. I'm giving you an opportunity. Tell me you love Me now. Feed My sheep. Follow Me!"

Don't worry about others by asking the Lord "What about them?" the way Peter did. Remember what He said to Peter: "What is that to you? You follow Me!"—another way of saying "That's none of your business. Look to Me, not them!" This is a great lesson. Don't focus on what others do. Don't be distracted by the way others are blessed or suffer.

You follow the path Jesus laid out for you!

APPENDIX

Theme of John:

SEGMENT DIVISIONS

PORTRAYALS OF JESUS CHRIST	SIGNS AND MIRACLES	MINISTRY	CHAPTER THEMES
		TO ISRAEL	1
			2
			3
			4
			5
			6
			7
			8
			9
			10
			11
		TO DISCIPLES	12
			13
			14
			15
			16
			17
		TO ALL MANKIND	18
			19
			20
		TO DISCIPLES	21

Author:

Date:

Purpose:

Key Words:
(including synonyms)

BIBLE CITIES IN THE TIME OF JESUS

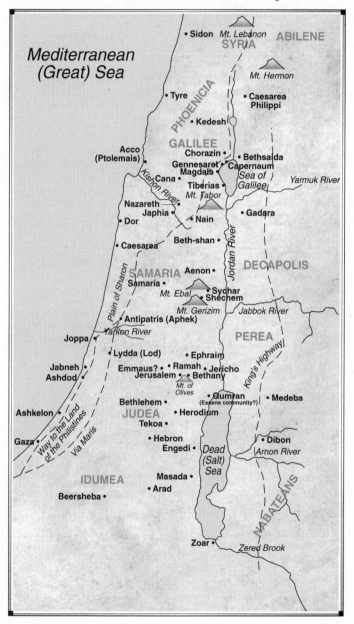

THE FEASTS OF ISRAEL

Slaves in Egypt	1st Month (Nisan) Festival of Passover (Pesach)				3rd Month (Sivan) Festival of Pentecost (Shavuot)
	Passover	Unleavened Bread	First fruits		Pentecost or Feast of Weeks
	Kill lamb & put blood on doorpost Exodus 12:6, 7	Purging of all leaven (symbol of sin)	Wave offering of sheaf (promise of harvest to come)		Wave offering of two loaves of leavened bread
	1st month, 14th day Leviticus 23:5	1st month, 15th day for 7 days Leviticus 23:6-8 (1st and 7th days are Sabbath)	Day after Sabbath Leviticus 23:9-14 (It is a Sabbath)		50 days after first fruits Leviticus 23:15-21 (It is a Sabbath)
Whosoever commits sin is the slave to sin	Christ our Passover has been sacrificed	Clean out old leaven... just as you are in fact unleavened	Christ has been raised...the first fruits	Going away so Comforter can come Mount of Olives	Promise of the Spirit, mystery of church: Jews-Gentiles in one body
John 8:34	1 Corinthians 5:7	1 Corinthians 5:7, 8	1 Corinthians 15:20-23	John 16:7 Acts 1:9-12	Acts 2:1-47 1 Corinthians 12:13 Ephesians 2:11-22

Months: Nisan—*March, April* • **Sivan**—*May, June* • **Tishri**—*September, October*

	7th Month (Tishri) Festival of Tabernacles *(Succoth)*			
	Feast of Trumpets	**Day of Atonement**	**Feast of Booths or Tabernacles**	
	Trumpet blown — a holy convocation	*Atonement shall be made to cleanse you* Leviticus 16:30	*Harvest celebration memorial of tabernacles in wilderness*	
Interlude Between Festivals	7th month, 1st day Leviticus 23:23-25 *(It is a Sabbath)*	7th month, 10th day Leviticus 23:26-32 *(It is a Sabbath)*	7th month, 15th day, for 7 days; 8th day, Holy Convocation Leviticus 23:33-44 *(The 1st and 8th days are Sabbaths)*	**New heaven and new earth**
	Regathering of Israel in preparation for final day of atonement Jeremiah 32:37-41	**Israel will repent and look to Messiah in one day** Zechariah 3:9,10; 12:10; 13:1; 14:9	**Families of the earth will come to Jerusalem to celebrate the Feast of Booths** Zechariah 14:16-19	**God tabernacles with men** Revelation 21:1-3
		Coming of Christ		
	Ezekiel 36:24	Ezekiel 36:25-27 Hebrews 9, 10 Romans 11:25-29	Ezekiel 36:28	

Israel had two harvests each year—spring and autumn

JERUSALEM OF THE NEW TESTAMENT

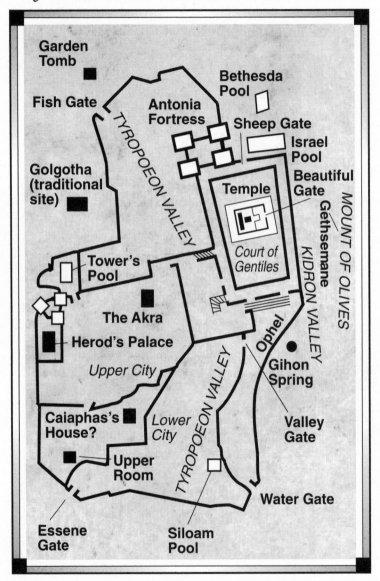

NOTES

1. KJV: miracle(s)
2. NIV: gives birth
3. KJV, NKJV: everlasting life
4. KJV, NKJV: everlasting life
5. KJV: miracle
6. KJV: quickeneth
7. KJV, NKJV: witness
8. KJV, NKJV, NIV: everlasting life
9. KJV: miracle
10. KJV: miracle
11. KJV: Christ
12. KJV: valid, right, reliable
13. KJV: miracle
14. KJV: putting their faith in
15. KJV: condemn
16. KJV: remain
17. KJV: true
18. KJV: true
19. KJV: returned
20. KJV, NKJV: first of all

Books in the
New Inductive Study Series

⁓⁓⁓⁓⁓

Teach Me Your Ways
Genesis, Exodus,
Leviticus, Numbers, Deuteronomy

Choosing Victory,
Overcoming Defeat
Joshua, Judges, Ruth

Desiring God's Own Heart
1 & 2 Samuel, 1 Chronicles

Walking Faithfully with God
1 & 2 Kings, 2 Chronicles

Overcoming Fear
and Discouragement
Ezra, Nehemiah, Esther

Trusting God
in Times of Adversity
Job

God's Answers for
Today's Problems
Proverbs

God's Blueprint
for Bible Prophecy
Daniel

Discovering the God
of Second Chances
Jonah, Joel, Amos, Obadiah

Finding Hope
When Life Seems Dark
Hosea, Micah, Nahum,
Habakkuk, Zephaniah

Opening the Windows
of Blessings
Haggai, Zechariah, Malachi

The Call to Follow Jesus
Luke

The God Who Cares
and Knows You
John

The Holy Spirit
Unleashed in You
Acts

God's Answers for
Relationships and Passions
1 & 2 Corinthians

Free from Bondage
God's Way
Galatians, Ephesians

That I May Know Him
Philippians, Colossians

Standing Firm in
These Last Days
1 & 2 Thessalonians

Walking in Power,
Love, and Discipline
1 & 2 Timothy, Titus

Living with Discernment
in the End Times
1 & 2 Peter, Jude

God's Love Alive in You
1, 2, & 3 John,
Philemon, James

Behold, Jesus Is Coming!
Revelation